ROBE
AND FIG)

PREVIOUSLY PUBLISHED
BY THE AUTHORS

Littleport in Old Picture Postcards
Strange Tales of East Anglia

Robber Barons
and Fighting Bishops

DEREK RICHINGS
AND ROGER RUDDERHAM

JOHN NICKALLS PUBLICATIONS

First published 2003

Cover illustration: *Bishop Longchamp*
An artist's impression by Gavin Rodrigues

ISBN 1 904136 14 1

Published by John Nickalls Publications,
Oak Farm Bungalow, Sawyers Lane, Suton,
Wymondham, Norfolk NR18 9SH

Designed by Ashley Gray and Printed by Geo R Reeve Ltd,
9–11 Town Green, Wymondham, Norfolk NR18 0BD

Contents

Preface

T HE MIDDLE AGES has always been a fascinating period of history, when the great Kings, such as William the Conqueror, Richard the Lionheart, and bad King John reigned over England. But while most people are aware of these great monarchs, the events that occurred in East Anglia during this period are not so familiar.

In this account we have endeavoured to give details of all the major events that occurred from the Norman Conquest to the signing of the Magna Carta. Also included are events which appear more legendary than historic fact, such as The Loathsome Hunters, and the Wild Man of Orford, but to the chroniclers who recorded the stories they were real, and we believe they add colour and mystery to those long ago days.

The quotes of the old chroniclers appearing now and again in the text are taken from the 19th century translations of the Chronicles of Hugh Candidas of Peterborough, Henry of Huntingdon, Roger of Wendover, and Jocelyn of Brakland. But for the patience and labour of these monkish scribes in devoting their time to recording the events and gossip of those days, our knowledge would be much the poorer today.

The remains of many of the castles and abbeys mentioned still exist, and a selection of recommended sites to visit are included at the end of the book.

Derek Richings
Roger Rudderham
2003

CHAPTER ONE

The Arrival of the Normans, 1066–1080

OMENS

The Medieval age was a time of many odd superstitions – almost anything that appeared slightly out of the ordinary would be considered as either a good or bad omen.

At dawn on the 28th September, 1066, William, Duke of Normandy, first set foot on English soil at Pevensey Bay. When he unfortunately slipped, falling face downwards onto the sandy beach, the superstitious amongst his army of 7,000 invading troops were gravely concerned – they regarded his fall as an ill-omen. But William, undeterred, is reported to have grabbed a handful of sand and cried: 'By the glory of God, I have taken possession of my kingdom! The soil of England is in my hands'.

When the news of the Norman invasion reached King Harold, who was celebrating his victory over the invading Norwegians at Stamford Bridge, near York, he immediately mustered his army and marched south. He allowed them only a short stay of rest upon reaching his manor of Waltham, Essex whilst he visited the church of the Holy Cross to pray.

Those who witnessed him kneel before the holy cross said that the figure of Christ gazed down upon him sadly, and they interpreted that as an ill-omen.

On the 14th October, only eight days after the supposed 'ill omen', King Harold lay amongst the many dead on Senlac Hill after his army was defeated in the bloody Battle of Hastings. Both sides sustained heavy losses. But the Norman cavalry and crossbowmen were superior to the English. Although Harold's army fought with vigour, his soldiers suffered the disadvantage of having to fight on foot, armed only with axes and shields.

Four days later, the victorious Duke William ordered one of his knights, William Malet, to search for the body of Harold, but the knight found it impossible to locate, so great was the slaughter.

It was left to King Harold's mistress, Edith Swan-Neck, to pick her way

The body of King Harold was secretly conveyed to Waltham and buried in the Priory Church. − LATE NINETEENTH CENTURY ILLUSTRATION.

through the gruesome mass of dead bodies and find Harold's mutilated corpse by recognising distinguishing marks that only she was aware of.

Edith pleaded with Duke William that her lover should be given a Christian burial, but the Duke was adamant that Harold's body should be unceremoniously buried on the seashore. But, Edith, with the connivance and help of the monks from Waltham Priory, secretly conveyed Harold's corpse to Waltham and buried it in front of the high altar in the Priory Church.

THE COLLABORATOR FROM CLAVERING
The infiltration of Normans and Bretons into England began during the reign of King Edward the Confessor. Half-Norman himself, Edward favoured Normans at his court and appointed seven of them to high positions, conferring upon them titles and lands of their own.

One such favoured foreigner was Robert FitzWimarc, who was a Breton by birth. Edward first made him a staller (a type of steward) at his court, then appointed him Sheriff of Essex in 1052.

The powerful position enabled Robert to accumulate vast areas of land in Essex from his seat in Clavering, where he built an enormous castle.

When news of Duke William's victory at Hastings reached Robert FitzWimarc, and also learned that the Conqueror was marching on London, Robert immediately rounded up all the able-bodied male Bretons and Normans living in the vicinity to assist the Duke in his plan to encircle London. Robert's mustered army encountered little resistance on the route to Greenwich, where they joined forces with Duke William, thus helping William to surround London and cut it off from its adjoining counties.

Realising there was no hope of receiving supplies of food, let alone assistance, the governing magnates of the city had little choice but to surrender.

Duke William consequently entered the city of London unopposed. He was crowned King of England at Westminster Abbey on Christmas Day, 1066.

Robert FitzWimarc's reward for actively supporting William in his quest to be king was to be officially appointed Sheriff of Essex under William's new regime. The position enabled him to accumulate more wealth and gain even greater power.

THE GOLDEN BOROUGH

Leofric, the Abbot of Peterborough, a firm supporter of King Harold, had been with the monarch on his stand against the Norman invasion, but had fallen ill before the fateful Battle of Hastings and was obliged to return to his home in Peterborough, where he died on the eve of the Feast of All Saints, November 1st. A chronicler of Peterborough, at the time, records that the Abbot was greatly mourned and bewailed by laymen and monks alike, and that few were agreeable to lower him into his tomb. But as revered as he was, there were certain people who had resented his power and wealth because, as a nephew of the Earl of Mercia, Leofric had been much loved and favoured by the old King Edward, who not only appointed him Abbot of Peterborough but also Abbot of Burton, Coventry, Thorney and Crowland.

The high position had enabled Leofric to build a large ecclesiastical empire. Much of the income, received from vast acres of land, went towards enriching the monasteries under his authority, especially the one situated at Peterborough, where he had lived in great splendour and luxury. Ornaments of gold and silver decorated the Abbey church, and a huge gold cross, encrusted with precious jewels, hanging above the high altar.

The symbols of such great wealth on display led to Peterborough being referred to by the Anglo-Saxons as Gildenburgh, meaning The Golden Borough.

When Abbot Leofric was finally laid to rest in his tomb, the monks elected

Effigy of a Saxon Abbot of Peterborough.

Brand the Prior to replace him because, according to the Anglo-Saxon Chronicle, 'he was a very good man and also wise'.

Brand was related to the nobles in Mercia and favoured the Saxon cause. He was reluctant to recognise the newly-crowned William as King of England, and applied to Edgar the Athling, the Saxon claimant to the throne, for official confirmation of his election.

The discourtesy infuriated William, whose anger was only appeased by a demand of 40 gold marks from the abbey. Brand was obliged to pay it, but the fine only increased his hatred of the Normans.

THE VICEROY

William the Conqueror returned to Normandy in February 1067 after appointing William FitzOsbern as viceroy over all captured lands north of the Thames.

FitzOsbern was a life-long friend of William and had been his steward in Normandy before the invasion. When that occurred, he was given command of the right wing of the invasion force and played a major role in the Normans' victory at the Battle of Hastings.

William rewarded him by giving him the Earldom of Hereford and vast estates on the Welsh borders.

As viceroy, FitzOsbern was entrusted to look after King William's interests, preserve order and discipline and suppress rebellion. Although the Norman forces were low in number, and the East Anglians seemed to have readily submitted to the Conqueror's rule, FitzOsbern was a ruthless warlord who was determined to maintain his authority by instilling fear into the population lest they should think of planning an uprising.

As a symbol of his power he decided to erect a castle at Norwich, and brutally evicted 113 residents from their homes and demolished their buildings because they were situated on his chosen site for the castle. He then forced the local population to work on the construction of its defensive earthworks.

FitzOsbern had command of a large force of soldiers, whose loyalty he maintained by drawing on King William's coffers to pay them extravagantly.

His stern rule in East Anglia brought a resigned peace to the region, but he was constantly menaced by the Welsh on the Western borders of his territory.

When Edric the Wild, a Mercian landowner, supported by his Welsh allies, rose in revolt and laid siege to Hereford Castle, FitzOsbern was forced to lead the bulk of his army to Hereford to quell the rebellion. They arrived just in time to save Hereford Castle from falling into the hands of the rebels.

THE FEARED TAX COLLECTOR

During his absence from East Anglia, FitzOsbern entrusted an obscure Norman knight, named Waleran, to safeguard Norwich Castle and look after Norman interests in the region.

Waleran had followed the Conqueror to England, more in the hope of gaining booty for himself rather than as an enthusiastic supporter of the invasion.

The official position he was eventually given by FitzOsbern is not recorded, but the widespread power he held suggests that he was most likely made Sheriff of the county. Whatever the office, he appears to have paid the King a fixed annual sum for the privilege of collecting the Royal taxes, exploiting the people mercilessly for his own ends.

Greedy and aggressive, Waleran ruthlessly relieved the people of their money. If they could not pay his demands he would confiscate their lands and houses. In this way he is said to have ruined several burgesses of Norwich, while others were forced to flee to Ipswich in order to escape his unjust exactions. One chronicler of the time recorded that 'the ancient and honourable families were reduced to beggary'.

He also became castellan of the newly erected castle at Colchester, and appears to have had the responsibility of extracting the Conqueror's oppressive taxes from the people of Essex. Here, as in Norfolk, he looted with impunity, turning a deaf ear to the people's complaints of his injustice.

In desperation, the people took their complaints to Athelmaer, Bishop of Elmham, who did what he could to ease their situation, but as a Saxon bishop he had little influence over a cruel and oppressive Norman. The people had to endure Waleran's reign of terror until the old tyrant died in 1075.

A NEW CHURCH FOR SAINT EDMUND

The most revered saint in East Anglia was St. Edmund, the last Saxon King of East Anglia, who suffered martyrdom at the hands of the Danes in A.D.870. The remains of the Saint were brought to the town of Bedericsworth in A.D.903, but it was not until a Benedictine Abbey was founded there in 1020 that his remains were transferred to the Abbey Church. Thereafter, the place became known as Bury St. Edmunds.

In 1050 a dumb woman, named Alfgeth, went on a pilgrimage to St.

Edmund's Shrine where she claimed to have miraculously recovered her speech. In gratitude to St. Edmund she stayed at the abbey and devoted her life to keeping the church and shrine clean and tidy.

One night St. Edmund appeared to her and told her that his coffin was being eaten by woodworms and that he wanted something done about it. At first Abbot Leofstan thought she was mad, but eventually gave in to her incessant demands and opened the tomb.

The coffin was found to be in a state of decay, but the body of the saint was perfectly preserved. Curious to know if the head was still attached to the body, Leofstan asked one of the monks to hold the feet while he tugged at the head. The moment he began to pull he suffered a stroke which left him dumb, blind and paralysed in the arms.

The shocked monks carried Leofstan from the scene, and St. Edmund's body was laid in a new coffin and replaced in his tomb.

When King Edward heard of the events he sent his personal physician, a French monk named Baldwin, to attend to the paralysed Abbot. Leofstan gradually recovered his sight and speech, probably by natural causes rather than from the medicinal administrations of Baldwin, but remained paralysed until his death in 1065. The monks of the abbey then elected Baldwin to be their abbot.

The Abbey of St. Edmund was well-endowed with lands and one of the richest in England. Baldwin, ambitious and anxious to make his mark on the abbey, decided that a new and grander church should be built; a church fit to hold the mortal remains and shrine of England's Patron Saint.

Immediately after Duke William had been proclaimed King, Baldwin, being a Frenchman, did not hesitate to seek favours from the new monarch.

The new King supported Baldwin's grand plan and issued orders to the Abbot of Peterborough to permit him to take sufficient stone from the quarries at Barnack for the erection of the new church at Bury, stipulating that Baldwin should be exempted from the usual tolls chargeable on the carriage of stone from that place.

The foundations were quickly laid, but the building work went on for many years.

DANISH RAIDERS AT ELY

Soon after his coronation in 1066, King Harold appointed a new abbot to the vacant monastery at Ely. The man chosen was Thurstan, a native of the nearby village of Witchford, who had been brought up in the monastery from childhood. He was considered to be a learned man who understood both English and Latin, and was highly regarded as 'a man of approved virtue and moderation'.

Moderation, however, was soon discarded when his benefactor King Harold was slain at Hastings. Thurstan, determined to resist the Conqueror, gave his support to Edgar the Athling, whom he considered the rightful heir to Harold, and readily gave shelter at the abbey to all enemies of King William who fled to the Isle of Ely for security.

Ely at that time was totally surrounded by water and marsh, accessible only by boat, and was thought to be a safe haven. In the autumn of 1068, a large force of Danes, under the command of Jarl Osbiorn, sailed up the River Ouse to Ely, where they were given a warm welcome by Abbot Thurstan and his rebel friends.

The Danes under Osbiorn were a comparatively small breakaway force from the main army under King Sweyn of Denmark which had pillaged and plundered its way to York. Thurstan, believing this resident force of Danes would ultimately reconquer the whole country and drive out the Normans, encouraged the people of the Fens to join them.

The Saxons soon found a natural leader in Hereward, a Saxon noble, who, having had an adventurous life in Flanders, returned home to find that his lands had been confiscated by the Normans and his brother killed in an attempt to defend the property. Hereward readily took command of the Saxons for the purpose of seeking revenge.

THE SACK OF PETERBOROUGH

On 27th November, 1069, Brand, the old Abbot of Peterborough, passed away. When King William heard the news he lost no time in appointing a Norman, Turold of Fecamp, to succeed him, not so much because he was a holy man, but because he possessed the qualities of a ruler and warrior, and William wanted strong Norman rule in that part of the rebellious Fens.

Turold, the former Abbot of Malmesbury, immediately set out for Peterborough with an army of 160 men to take possession of his prestigious abbey.

The news of Turold's arrival at Stamford, precipitated a crisis. Hereward, who was a nephew of the late Abbot Brand, anxious that the treasures the Saxons had bestowed upon the abbey should not fall into the hands of the Normans, invited the Danes to help transport the treasures of Peterborough to a place of safety.

The monks, alarmed when they saw the Danes approaching, closed the monastery gates, and 'courageously began to defend from above'. A strenuous battle was fought, but Hereward and the Danes were unable to force an entry. They then set fire to the building adjoining the gates which finally allowed them to gain entry into the monastery.

Once inside the monastery the Danes began an orgy of looting. They

Once inside the Abbey of Peterborough the Danes began an orgy of looting.

carried off everything of gold and silver to their boats, except the great gold cross, which was too heavy for them. Nevertheless, they stripped it of its jewels and took the gold crown from the head of Christ.

After they had stripped the monastery of everything of value, they returned to their boats and set sail for the safety of the Isle of Ely.

When Abbot Turold arrived with his army he found his monastery a smouldering ruin, the great church burned down, and only one sick monk to greet him, the others having fled or been taken hostage by the Danes.

THE CAMP OF REFUGE

The Danes never had the intention of making a full-scale invasion of England, and in the summer of 1070 a treaty was drawn up between King Sweyn of Denmark and King William which allowed King Sweyn to evacuate his army out of England. The Danes had been interested only in loot, which they gladly took with them.

Jarl Osbiorn collected his treasures, plundered from the monastery of Peterborough, and set sail with his fleet up the River Ouse for his homeland. All went well until they were halfway across the North Sea. A violent storm suddenly blew up and scattered the fleet. Some ships ended up in Norway, some as far away as Ireland, while others were lost altogether with their cargo of treasure.

The departure of the Danes from England must have been a disappointment for Abbot Thurstan and his growing band of rebels. The news of Hereward's success in sacking Peterborough brought many prominent Saxons, who were opposed to William's rule, to the Isle of Ely.

Among those who sought refuge with the Abbot were Athelwine, Bishop of Durham, Morcar, Earl of Northumberland, Frithric, Abbot of St. Alban's, and Siward, a Northumbrian thane.

Hereward was considered the leader of the rebel gathering. For almost a year they fortified the island of Ely and held out in defiance of their Norman overlords. Their guerrilla raids into the surrounding countryside were at first considered more of a nuisance than a threat, but in late 1071 King William decided that resistance to his rule could no longer be tolerated or ignored.

He gathered his forces together and marched on Ely.

THE SIEGE OF ELY

A full assault on the Island of Ely was impossible because of the water and marsh surrounding it. The chronicler Florence of Worcester recounts that the King 'blocked up every outlet on the eastern side of the island by his sailors'. But the blockade, intended to starve out the rebels, was ineffective as the monks had built up a vast supply of food.

The King then moved the bulk of his army to Aldreth 'where the least water and marsh surrounded the Isle'. Here he commanded that a bridge or causeway should be constructed across the marsh to the Isle.

The Normans began the task by binding tree trunks together. Beneath the tree trunks they placed sheepskins inflated with air, so that the causeway would carry the weight of soldiers in full chain mail.

Hereward and his rebels took every opportunity to make sudden forays to hinder their progress during the construction. The delays are said to have made the King 'excessively angry'.

But the causeway was eventually completed and the first serious assault on the Isle began.

The attack was led by William Malet, a Norman baron who had been given vast estates in Suffolk, including the Lordship of Eye, for his services at Hastings.

It was said that 'a great multitude of men rushed upon it, eager, among other things, to get gold and silver which they thought to be plentifully hidden in the Isle'.

The sudden weight of heavily armed soldiers de-stabilised the causeway and it gave way, plunging many to their deaths in the deep watery swamp.

Observing the plight of the Normans, Hereward and his men ventured out from behind their defences and showered them with arrows. The Normans were killed in great numbers, including their leader, William Malet, who fell mortally wounded by a Saxon arrow.

King William had watched his army perish in the swamp with 'heartfelt sorrow', and departed for his castle at Cambridge, 'laying aside all hope of making any further attack on the Isle'.

He did, however, leave the remainder of his army to guard the Isle on all sides to prevent the rebels leaving the safety of their defences to lay waste to the surrounding district.

BETRAYAL

Conquering the Island of Ely had proved to be a more formidable task for King William than conquering the English at Hastings and claiming the throne. For several months the Isle was blockaded, William had hoped that

Hereward and his band of rebels fled the Isle of Ely after their defeat in 1071. – COURTESY OF THE CAMBRIDGESHIRE COLLECTION.

Hereward returned to England, paid homage to King William, and was restored to his lands. – COURTESY OF THE CAMBRIDGESHIRE COLLECTION.

shortage of food would eventually force the rebels to capitulate. Abbot Thurstan, realising the hopeless position they were in and fearful of the King's wrath and vengeance, decided to negotiate with the Normans secretly.

He sent messengers from the Isle to treat with the King, hoping to bring the stalemate to a bloodless end. The monks agreed to convey the Norman army across the marsh by boat and show them a secret way into the monastery.

But a monk, by the name of Alwinus, informed Hereward of the Abbot's betrayal and that Thurstan had made a covenant with the King. Hereward was furious and would have set fire to the monastery and destroyed it, had he not been informed that the Norman army had already entered the Isle.

Hereward rallied the Saxons, who repelled the invaders several times, but were forced to retreat after a final courageous battle, in which a great number were slaughtered.

Hereward managed to secure a boat and, with a handful of rebels, fled north across the Littleport Fens, setting fire to the reeds and sedge grass to cover their escape.

Victory was declared by the jubilant King William, whose punishment of the rebels was swift and merciless. Many were blinded, others had their hands and feet cut off as a warning to those who dared to incur the King's displeasure.

Earl Morcar and Siward were transported to Normandy, where they were imprisoned for life. The Bishop of Durham was locked away in the monastery at Abingdon for the remainder of his days.

Abbot Thurstan was summoned before the King, whose intention was to depose him, but the wily old abbot's prudent conduct impressed the King to the point where Thurstan was pardoned of all transgressions and allowed to continue governing the abbey, although the monastery was forced to pay a fine of 1,000 gold marks and operate under the watchful eye of a contingent of forty Norman soldiers until Thurstan's death.

After Thurstan's demise, the King lost no time in sending his officials to seize all the gold and silver plate from the monastery and take it to his own treasury. He then appointed a Norman, Theodwine of Jumiege as Abbot, but when Theodwine arrived in Ely to discover that the monastery had been stripped of all its wealth, he refused to accept the position until the treasures were returned to their rightful place.

The King, anxious to resolve the Ely problems, reluctantly agreed, and returned the treasure to Ely.

Hereward was outlawed and remained in exile on the continent for a few years. He eventually returned to England and submitted to King William, who restored Hereward to his land and title.

BISHOP VERSUS ABBOT

Having established his authority over most of England, King William began to depose many Saxon clerics and officials and replace them with trusted Normans. In 1070 he ended the 23 year reign of Athelmaer, Bishop of East Anglia, by deposing him and appointed his chaplain, Herfast, a monk from the Abbey of Bec in Normandy, to succeed him.

Herfast was also given the position of Chancellor – the first person in England to hold the title. He was, however, disliked and even despised in many quarters, being looked down upon as 'a man of slender ability and moderate learning'.

Like his predecessor, Herfast was a married man and preferred the luxury of court life to that of a provincial bishop. He naturally preferred married clergy and ordained several married men into the priesthood, thus incurring the displeasure of Lanfranc, the Archbishop of Canterbury, who admonished him for his 'clerical laxity'.

The Archbishop had known Herfast since the days when they were both monks at the Abbey of Bec, and took a dislike to him for his arrogant and haughty manner. He was no great scholar and was considered ignorant by the Archbishop, who ordered him to 'devote less time to gambling and games of chance, and to read the Bible and learn some Canon Law'.

The Cathedral of East Anglia was at that time a modest Saxon church, situated at North Elmham, which Herfast considered unsuitable for such a large diocese. A monkish chronicler recorded that Herfast 'decided to go down in posterity as a man who had done something'.

He set his sights on the magnificent new church under construction at Bury St. Edmunds, and decided that it would be his new cathedral. As Bishop of East Anglia he had jurisdiction over all the abbeys in the region, so it seemed there was nothing to stop him carrying out his plan.

When Baldwin, the Abbot of Bury St Edmunds, heard of the bishop's intention he resolved to oppose the move, claiming that the abbey and its lands were exempt from diocesan jurisdiction according to a charter it held.

Herfast consequently refused to accept opposition to his authority, and he and Baldwin engaged in a long and obstinate dispute, until they both appealed to the King in desperation to resolve it.

The King sent Archbishop Lanfranc to East Anglia to arbitrate, but Lanfranc was taken ill when he reached Freckenham in Suffolk, and Baldwin, who was also a renowned physician, was called to his bedside.

Lanfranc soon recovered and continued his journey to Bury St. Edmunds. When he arrived at the abbey he pondered and deliberated the case for some time, and eventually gave an uncommitted judgement that appeared to favour Abbot Baldwin, but this satisfied neither side. The dispute was therefore referred to Rome for the Pope to give judgement.

The two men had to wait anxiously until 1074 before Pope Gregory finally came to a decision and sent a letter to Archbishop Lanfranc favouring Baldwin. When Herfast received the letter from the Archbishop informing him of the Pope's decision he was so angry that he violently struck the messenger who brought him the news.

In 1075 a council in London decreed that English bishops should transfer their sees from villages to towns. Herfast complied with this by moving his bishopric from North Elmham to Thetford, where the great Church of St. Mary became the cathedral of the East Anglian diocese.

THE BRIDE-ALE PLOT

Gyrth Godwinson, the Earl of East Anglia, had fallen, with his brother King Harold, at the Battle of Hastings, and the title remained vacant until 1068, when King William appointed Ralph the Staller, a Breton, to the position. Ralph had served King Edward the Confessor faithfully during his reign but was now a loyal supporter of the Norman King.

When Ralph the elder died two years later he was succeeded by his son, Ralph Guader, who was also made Constable of the Royal castle at Norwich.

Ralph the younger had been outlawed by King Harold, but returned to England with the Conqueror and fought for him at the Battle of Hastings in the army of Count Alan of Brittany, and became a loyal subject of King William until he fell in love with and sought permission to marry Lady Emma, the daughter of the late William FitzOsbern, Earl of Hereford and builder of Norwich Castle.

For reasons unknown, King William opposed the marriage and forbade it to take place. Heedless of the King's order, Ralph married Emma and held a sumptuous banquet at a palace at Exning, near Newmarket. The guests included the bride's brother Roger, Earl of Hereford, Waltheof, the Saxon Earl of Huntingdon, Wulfcetel, Abbot of Crowland, and many other important barons and clerics along with several Welshmen invited by the Earl of Hereford. As the wine flowed freely, tongues became loosened and expressed grievances against the oppressive rule of King William. The more wine they drank, the more they talked and the bolder they became. Eventually, they all agreed that the bastard from Normandy should be removed from the throne and that the kingdom should be divided between them, even electing one of them to be king.

The three Earls then hatched a plan for three simultaneous rebellions to depose the despised monarch, Roger leading the one in the West, Ralph the one in the East, and Waltheof the one in the North.

After the guests at the banquet had dispersed, the Earls departed to raise their armies, no doubt having a final tipple before they left. Earl Ralph moved near Cambridge to gather his forces, whilst his bride, Lady Emma, went to Norwich to garrison the castle.

THE SIEGE OF NORWICH CASTLE

King William was out of the country at the time, quelling a rebellion in his continental domains, and Earl Waltheof, who was married to the King's niece, had second thoughts about the rebellion in sober reflection. He treacherously divulged the plot to Archbishop Lanfranc, who was Guardian of the Realm during the King's absence.

The Archbishop swiftly dispatched an army to East Anglia, under the joint command of the King's half-brother Odo, Bishop of Bayeux, and Geoffrey, Bishop of Coustances. They encountered the rebel army encamped near Cambridge. Both bishops were experienced military commanders, and although the battle was long and hard fought, the conspirators were eventually completely defeated. Hundreds were killed and hundreds more taken prisoner.

As a punishment for their treachery each prisoner of whatever rank had his right foot amputated.

Earl Ralph escaped from the field of battle and fled to Norwich Castle, the two bishops with their army in hot pursuit, killing and maiming any rebels they encountered on their way.

But by the time the two bishops arrived at Norwich, Ralph had set sail for Denmark to seek help from England's old enemy, King Sweyn, leaving his wife, Lady Emma, and her loyal supporters to hold out in the castle until help arrived.

For three long months they withstood the siege, but help never came. Although the castle seemed impregnable, the town suffered badly, and eventually the threat of famine forced Emma to come to terms with the bishops.

She was given 40 days to leave the realm, and joined her husband, Ralph, in Brittany, where they lived the rest of their lives in their castle, banished from England as outlaws. All their lands and property in East Anglia were forfeited.

Earl Roger's rebellion in the west was also suppressed, and he was captured and imprisoned in Normandy for the rest of his life.

THE EARL OF HUNTINGDON'S HEAD

On the advice of Archbishop Lanfranc, Waltheof went to Normandy to make his peace with King William. But the King was angered by the Earl's implication in plotting the rebellion, despite the fact that he had confessed the details in full to Lanfranc and was not involved in military action.

Waltheof had been involved in a previous rebellion and King William was not in a forgiving mood, deciding that the man was untrustworthy and could not be given a third chance.

As an Englishman, Waltheof was subject to English law, under which treason was punishable by death. After being imprisoned for some months, Waltheof was beheaded at Winchester on 31st May 1076.

According to tradition, Waltheof was reciting the Lord's Prayer and had murmured the words 'and lead us not into temptation', just as the axe fell. The severed head was then heard to say in a loud voice; "But deliver us from evil. Amen."

Abbot Wulfcetel, who had also been present at the Bride-ale plot gathering, conveyed the decapitated body of the Earl to his abbey at Crowland where it was buried in the Chapter House.

It was not long before supposed miracles began to occur, and the abbey became the centre of a cult venerating Waltheof as a saint.

Angered that a traitor should be so venerated, King William accused

Ely Cathedral under construction in the late 11th century – COURTESY OF THE
CAMBRIDGESHIRE COLLECTION.

Wulfcetel of preaching that Waltheof was a saint, then deposed the abbot and
imprisoned him in Glastonbury Abbey, but the cult of Waltheof continued for
several centuries.

ABBOT SIMEON'S CHURCH

The monastery at Ely suffered badly after the defeat of Hereward. Its
treasures were plundered, and several local magnates took the opportunity to
seize its lands. Thus its once considerable income was greatly reduced.

To add to its financial troubles, the King garrisoned forty soldiers at the
monastery, one for each monk, to ensure it never again became the centre of
rebellion.

After the death of Theodwine, the first Norman Abbot of Ely, on 4th
December 1075, a successor was not appointed for seven years. A monk
called Godfrey was nominated to govern the abbey. With its income greatly
reduced, and the added burden of the upkeep of forty knights to meet, the
monastery became neglected and its financial state precarious.

Godfrey, however, who was unofficially regarded as Abbot, proved to be an
able and efficient administrator, and petitioned the King for restoration of all
the lands, rights and liberties of the monastery.

The King's displeasure with the monks of Ely eventually mellowed, and he
directed his half-brother, Odo, Bishop of Bayeux, to summon the chief barons

of East Anglia to an assembly held at Kentford, near Newmarket, on 2nd April 1080, to establish just where the lands belonging to the abbey lay.

After extensive investigation and much deliberation, the assembly adjudged that all the possessions, rights, customs and privileges of the Church of Ely, which it held in the time of Edward the Confessor, should be fully restored.

A year after the assembly took place, Godfrey was promoted as Abbot of Malmesbury, the King at last appointing a new Abbot of Ely, Simeon, previously Prior of Winchester, and brother of Walkelin, the Bishop of Winchester.

Simeon was more than eighty years of age, but was surprisingly energetic. He successfully recovered the abbey's lands from the powerful barons who were reluctantly obliged to give them up.

When Simeon had been Prior of Winchester, his brother, the bishop, had begun building a splendid cathedral in the town. Determined not to be outdone, Simeon decided to build a church at Ely that would equal if not surpass his brother's in magnificence.

He devoted a considerable part of his personal fortune to the project, even though he knew, at his advanced age, that he would never live to see the building completed .

Even so, he lived for twelve more years to oversee the work, sometimes from his sick bed as the infirmities of old age overcame him. How far the work had progressed when Simeon died in 1093 is difficult to say, but it is possible that the east end of the cathedral, including the apse, choir, north transept and central tower had been completed, closely following the design of Winchester Cathedral.

CHAPTER TWO

The Domesday Survey, 1080–1087

SYMBOLS OF OPPRESSION

By 1075 King William, having crushed all his opponents, and to ensure peace and security continued, carried out a programme of either building castles in almost every county town, or improving the appearance of existing ones.

The castles of earth and timber, generally termed motte and bailey, consisted of a large earth mound, on top of which was placed a wooden keep overlooking a courtyard enclosed by an embankment topped with a wooden palisade. This type of castle was quickly constructed and intended to overawe the Saxons and remind them of who ruled the kingdom.

A castle had been constructed at Cambridge in 1068 outside the town commanding the River Cam crossing. The land on which it was built had been forcibly taken from the local peasants, and 27 of their homes had been demolished. Likewise, several Saxon houses had been demolished at Huntingdon to make way for the castle, where it was situated in an imposing position close to the River Ouse to control an important crossing point.

At Colchester a stone castle was begun about 1076. Its keep was built on the foundations of a Roman temple, and many of the materials used were salvaged from the temple's remains.

The keep followed closely the design of the Tower of London, only on a much grander scale. It was of massive proportions, measuring 191 feet by 110 feet. It rose to a height of 80 feet, and the walls were 12 feet thick, making it the largest Norman keep in England.

Colchester Castle and the Tower of London were probably designed by the same architect, a cleric named Gandalf, who shortly afterwards was appointed Bishop of Rochester.

In general, the county sheriff acted as custodian of the respective Royal Castle, although the King occasionally appointed a constable as guardian. Sheriffs exercised considerable powers in matters which concerned the

William the Conqueror erected a castle at Colchester soon after establishing his authority over England. – LATE NINETEENTH CENTURY POSTCARD PRINTED BY BENHAM & CO.

crown. They presided over the county, collected the royal taxes, and enforced military service.

The early sheriffs were often minor nobles or knights who had fought with the Conqueror at Hastings, and, greedy for land and wealth, were prepared to pay large amounts to the King to hold their position. Once they knew the position was secure, they abused their power by imposing extortionate taxes and seizing land from those who could not pay. In this way they made enormous profits, and many became powerful land owners in their particular county.

The sheriffs and the Royal Castles, from which they ruled ruthlessly, consequently became symbols of oppression to the Saxons.

THE GREAT SURVEY

The King rewarded his loyal supporters with vast estates which had once belonged to Saxon nobles, who had either been killed at Hastings or forcibly expelled merely because they were Saxons.

The remainder of the once-proud people of the country were reduced to peasants and serfs under the new social order imposed by the Conqueror. Under his feudal system, the King owned all the land and his Norman nobles held the estates he 'gave' them as tenants-in-chief, after they had sworn an oath of obedience to him.

They were given grand titles of Earl or Baron and were permitted to build a castle in the chief manor of their estate, on condition they supplied the King with knights in time of war, and garrison his royal castles.

The same obligations applied to bishops and abbots, who were regarded as ecclesiastical barons. The Abbot of Bury St. Edmunds, for instance, was obliged to keep 40 knights to garrison Norwich Castle, ten at a time, for a quarter of the year. But it became more common for the church to offer money instead of knights.

At Christmas 1085, almost twenty years after he had conquered England, King William held a great council at Gloucester for the purpose of ascertaining how much land he owned, how it was held and who his tenants were.

After a lengthy consultation, William dismissed the court with instructions that commissioners must be sent into all the counties of England to gather detailed accounts of every village and manor within its bounds. The inhabitants were obliged to answer such questions as to the size and use of the land, the number and status of the workers, the number of ploughteams, the number of mills and fishponds, how much was meadow and woodland, and how much the whole was worth. The survey was not merely for assessing tax, it also proved useful in disputes over rights to the lands, the purpose being that 'every man should know his right and not usurp another's'.

It took less than twelve months for the commissioners to complete the survey. It was carried out in such minute detail that it soon acquired the name Domesday, as it was thought to be similar to the kind of inquiry that would be made on the Day of Judgement.

THE GREATEST SHEEPMASTER IN ESSEX

One of the most affluent tenants-in-chief in Essex was Sweyn, the son of Robert FitzWimarc, who held a total of 66 manors, forty of which were grouped in the south of the county between the Rivers Thames and Crouch.

When his father died, he succeeded him to the office of Sheriff of Essex, he then abandoned the old castle at Clavering, building a new one at Rayleigh, which overlooked his lands on the Essex marshes, where he also established a large park and vineyard.

Sweyn owned thousands of acres of pasture on the Essex salt marshes, and it was here that he decided to concentrate his main interest, breeding sheep on a large scale.

The breeding and raising of sheep was a lucrative investment for those who could afford the initial outlay. Live sheep provided wool, milk, cheese, and manure for fertiliser. When killed, valuable parchment was produced from their skins, and their meat was always in demand.

The long-haired breed, favoured in East Anglia, produced a lush wool that was sought all over Europe, and as Sweyn maintained a flock of 4,000 sheep, he not only gained the reputation of being 'The greatest Sheepmaster in Essex', but also amassed a vast fortune.

Not content with this, his position as Sheriff enabled him to acquire more manors in every part of Essex to extend his pasturage, either by fair means or foul, to breed his valuable sheep.

Certainly not known as a generous man, he made an exception by giving his manor in Whatley to Westminster Abbey, probably with the ulterior motive of being buried there, for he died shortly afterwards in about 1100 and was laid to rest in the abbey.

THE LORD AND LADY OF ACRE

One very ambitious knight who took an active part in the Battle of Hastings was William de Warenne, whose zeal and devotion to Duke William earned him considerable rewards. He was given the Rape of Lewes in Sussex, 139 manors in Norfolk and 15 in Suffolk; as well as considerable lands in Surrey and Yorkshire.

He built castles at Lewes in Sussex, Reigate in Surrey, and at Acre in Norfolk. Acre, which lay in the fertile and richly-wooded valley of the River Nar, was his chief manor in Norfolk; and the magnificent castle he built there became his main residence in East Anglia.

When they visited their East Anglian estates, William and his wife, Lady Gundrada, could live in luxury and comfort in the two storey manor house erected on the large motte of the castle, which, together with the enormous bailey, covered seven acres of land.

William de Warenne became one of the wealthiest and most powerful barons in the country. Having fought against Hereward and his rebels in the Isle of

William de Warenne fought with the Conqueror at Hastings, and was well rewarded. – STAINED GLASS WINDOW IN CHURCH OF LEWES.

29

William de Warenne established a priory for the Cluniac Order at Castle Acre. – LATE NINETEENTH CENTURY POSTCARD

Ely in 1071, the King appointed him Chief Justice of England four years later, giving him authority to act on the King's behalf when the monarch was absent abroad.

In the same year he took part in the siege of Norwich during the rebellion of Earl Ralph. Having quelled the rebellion, de Warenne and Lady Gundrada decided to set off on a pilgrimage to Rome in 1076, but had travelled no further than Burgundy when they heard that war had broken out between the Pope and the Holy Roman Emperor.

Consequently, their visit to Rome never took place, but they made the most of their stay in Burgundy by visiting the great Abbey of Cluny. The reception they received in the abbey, and the experience they encountered, impressed them so much that they determined to establish a house dedicated to the Clunaic Order upon return to England.

Thus, the Priory of Lewes was founded in 1078 for the support of twelve monks. About six years later de Warenne started to build another priory near his castle at Acre, but the foundation stone had hardly been laid when Lady Gundrada died at Acre Castle on the 27th May 1085.

Her body was conveyed to Lewes, where it was buried in the Priory Church. It is said that the bereaved baron spent the remainder of his days in seclusion lamenting the loss of his beloved wife, devoting much of his time to religion, and to the priories that he and Gundrada had founded.

THE PROWLING WOLF

After the defeat of Hereward, many of the scattered lands of the Abbey of Ely were seized by rapacious barons with the sole interest of increasing their estates.

One such baron, who grasped the opportunity to seize whatever he could, was Picot, the harsh and unpopular Sheriff of Cambridgeshire.

Picot was a Norman knight, who came to England in the service of the Conqueror. He was given the barony of Bourn in Cambridgeshire, in recognition of his allegiance, and it is said that he ranked as an Earl.

Whatever his high rank, Picot was ruthless in his attempt to increase his wealth and power. He erected a castle at Bourn, which became his chief residence, and rode around the Shire with an escort of bodyguards, collecting extortionate taxes, rents and tolls, and terrorising the common people so that none dare raise their voice in complaint.

At Cambridge, he turned several families out of their houses, which were then demolished, in order to erect mills. He forced the people to take all their grain to his mills for grinding. Having monopolised milling, he illegally took away the people's rights to graze their cattle upon common pasture, and demanded the loan of their ploughs nine times a year for use on his own lands.

The elderly Abbot Simeon of Ely was disturbed by Picot's behaviour and waged an unrelenting campaign against him, probably spurred on by the monks of the abbey, who likened Picot to 'a prowling wolf, a crafty fox, a greedy hog'.

Determined to regain the abbey's stolen lands, Simeon eventually succeeded in forcing the 'shameless dog to disgorge his ill-gotten gains' and return them to the abbey.

EUSTACE THE SHERIFF

At the same time as Picot was terrorising the people of Cambridgeshire, Eustace de Lovetot, his counterpart in the neighbouring county of Huntingdonshire, was behaving just as rapaciously.

He had been given the barony of Southoe, which consisted of small parcels of land, but acquired much more property by misusing his powers, frequently disregarding legal procedure. Like Picot, he took advantage of Ely Abbey's misfortunes and seized many of its Huntingdonshire possessions, which he illegally held for five years until he was forced to give them back.

The misdeeds of Eustace, particularly when he was appointed Sheriff of the county, are too numerous to mention, but an example of his greed and lack of concern for others can be gleaned from his treatment of the widow of the previous sheriff, who had been granted a house in Huntingdon by King William where she could spend the rest of her days in peace.

Eustace claimed the house for himself, and having no respect for the law, or the King himself, turned the helpless widow out of her home and took possession of it.

He also appears to have had little more respect for the church, because he had no scruples in turning Godric, the priest of Weston, out of his house and seizing his lands.

But as Eustace grew older the weight of his sins began to play on his mind, and fearful that he would be condemned to hell, he founded a priory at Huntingdon for canons regular of the order of St. Augustine.

When he died, perhaps as a final atonement for his misdeeds, he endowed the priory with a substantial portion of his ill-gotten gains.

THE KNIGHT FROM LA MANCHE

Aubrey de Vere, a knight from the village of Ver in the La Manche region of Normandy, joined the invasion force of Duke William, no doubt eager to have his share of the promised spoils.

His valour at the Battle of Hastings earned him favour with the Conqueror, who rewarded him with lands in Essex, which were confiscated from Ulwine, the Saxon thane. Aubrey was also given lands in London and Kensington. At the time of the Great Survey, de Vere owned 14 manors in Essex, 9 in Suffolk, 7 in Cambridgeshire, 2 in Huntingdon, and some in Northamptonshire.

He chose the village of Hedingham in Essex as the seat of his barony, where he built a castle on a hilltop overlooking the River Colne.

The staple beverage of the Saxons at this time was beer, or ale, which was in plentiful supply in keeping with local demand. The Normans, however, preferred wine, which was scarce and not easy to obtain. To provide himself with wine in the future, and no doubt market it, Aubrey established vineyards in Hedingham, Belchamp and at his Suffolk manor of Lavenham.

The grapevines were brought over from his native land, and the largest of his vineyards was situated at Belchamp, a few miles north of Hedingham. It covered 11 arpents – an old French measure of land – which was roughly 17 acres, but the vines were slow to grow, either because of inclement weather or because the soil was unsuitable. At the time of the Great Survey, only a few vines in one arpent were recorded as producing fruit.

Aubrey also kept large flocks of sheep on his estates. One flock was pastured on land held by the King in the village of Abington in Cambridgeshire. The other half of the King's land in Abington was occupied by Picot the Sheriff, and when Aubrey needed to extend his pasture to accommodate more sheep, he decided to annex part of Sheriff Picot's land.

Picot, angered at Aubrey's high-handed action, challenged the seizure of the land in the Hundred Court, making sure that the court was rigged in his favour. Not surprisingly, the court's verdict was against Aubrey, whose response was to annex another slice of Picot's land.

The infuriated sheriff once again summoned a Hundred Court to judge the dispute, but the verdict was obviously weighted against Aubrey.

Regardless of his many powers, and his use and abuse of the Hundred Court, Picot failed to force Aubrey from his lands. Picot had seized so many unfortunate people's lands without consideration, that it seemed only just that he should have a taste of his own bitter medicine.

THE HONOUR OF CLARE

When King William dispossessed the Saxon nobles of their lands, the Suffolk estates of Earl Aluric were given to Richard FitzGilbert, Count of Brionne, as his share of the spoils for his loyalty and support during the invasion.

FitzGilbert was a descendent of Duke Richard I of Normandy, and a distant relative of King William. As such, he was determined to acquire much more land, and used his influence to obtain it.

In total he eventually received 170 lordships, scattered over ten counties, 95 of which were in Suffolk, and several in Kent, where he was given the Lordship of Tonbridge.

He chose the village of Clare, nestling in the fertile valley of the River Stow, as the seat of his barony, or Honour as it was known. Clare was chiefly an agricultural settlement before the Conquest, but by the time the Great Survey was made it had grown to the status of a market town, being one of the seven boroughs in Suffolk, with a population of about 600 people who were governed by 43 burgesses.

FitzGilbert established a timber motte and bailey castle near the River Stow, on the site of an old Saxon fort, as his chief residence and administrative centre for his East Anglian Honour.

The Great Survey records that FitzGilbert kept 12 hives of bees in his grounds, and no doubt he was responsible for establishing vineyards on 9 acres of land near his castle.

It has been claimed that the honeyed wine, known as Clary, acquired it name from the town of Clare, but the claim has never been proven.

THE TYRANNICAL 'WOODCUTTER'

Ivo Taillbois, whose surname literally translates as 'Woodcutter,' was said to have been a nephew of the Conqueror, and had acted as his standard-bearer during the Battle of Hastings.

He certainly seems to have been well-rewarded by the King for his services with lordships in Norfolk and Lincolnshire, where the majority of his estates were concentrated.

The abbey church of Ely dominated the surrounding flat Fenland, a visible symbol of the abbot's authority over the area. – LATE NINETEENTH CENTURY POSTCARD.

In 1071 he married Lucy, the daughter of Thurold, Sheriff of Lincoln, and was given the Lordship of Spalding, a small market town on the edge of the Fens in Lincolnshire.

He and his bride chose to reside in a castle built on the ridge of silt, which then formed the coastline of The Wash. He held court in the castle with great pomp, and would never allow a Saxon to approach him unless he did so on bended knees.

An old chronicler records that he had no love for the local people, 'but tortured, harried, worried and annoyed them every day with burdens'.

But it was the monks of Spalding Priory that aroused his hatred and fury most of all, for no other reason than that they were Saxons occupying the priory and its lands.

He did everything he could think of to terrorise them into quitting the priory, daily impounding their sheep, laming their cattle, oxen and horses, killing their swine and pigs, and driving their straying sheep into treacherous marshland with his dogs.

Every time he saw monks or servants of the Prior on the highway, he assaulted them with swords and staves. The situation became so unbearable that the monks eventually fled from the priory to their mother house, the nearby Abbey of Crowland, with all their movable possessions.

In about 1085, Ivo, who had by then succeeded his father-in-law as Sheriff of Lincoln, gave the priory of Spalding to the Abbey of St. Nicholas in his hometown of Angers in Anjou, and offered to provide land for the support of six monks of Angevin or Norman origin.

The Abbot of Angers accepted the offer, and to support the monks Ivo seized all the lands in Spalding belonging to the Abbey of Crowland.

The Abbot of Crowland challenged the legality of the seizures in the manor court, and produced charters to prove that Spalding had been founded as a cell of Crowland and that Ivo had no right to claim the lands, let alone give the priory to the Abbey of Angers.

Ivo claimed that the charters were forged, and tried to belittle them because they were written in Saxon, saying that 'such barbarous writing was only worthy of laughter and derision'. He even attempted to ambush the Crowland monks to steal the charters, but his attempt failed.

But the case never seems to have been proven either way at the time, for Crowland's attempt to recover their rights and lands was in vain, and the Priory of Spalding remained firmly under the control of the Abbot of Angers.

THE ISLAND OF EELS

The monastery of Ely, isolated by swamp and marsh, was refounded in 970, having lain in ruins for a hundred years after the Danes destroyed it in 870. The island of Ely covered an area seven miles in length and five in breadth.

Over the years the re-established monastery thrived, and at the time of the Great Survey, was recorded as owning a vast amount of land in East Anglia. Indeed the Abbot's lands were scattered over every county in the region, and were collectively known as the Honour of St. Etheldreda.

The name Ely derived from the Saxon word for eel, and the word Ely translates as the Island of Eels, eels being caught in plenty from the murky waters of the surrounding Fens. The Ely Chronicle, Liber Eliensis, records that there were 'netted innumerable eels, water wolves, pikerels, perch, roach, burbots and lampreys, together with the royal fish, the sturgeon'.

Fishing became one of the most important and profitable industries on the Abbot's Fenland manors. Many of the manors were obliged to supply the monastery with an annual quota of eels, which were caught in the summer in large bottle-shaped taps made of osiers.

The manor of Littleport was directed to supply 17,000 eels each year, Stuntney 24,000 eels, and Doddington, the largest amount of 27,150 eels. The Abbot also employed two fishermen at Wisbech who rendered him 14,000 eels a year.

The eels and fish were preserved in salt from the salt-pans in the manor of

Terrington, for the sustenance of the monks during the winter months, but they were by no means the only fayre on the refectory table.

Mutton, pork, beef, bread, butter, cheese and honey, were also available in plenty, and the Abbot, who ranked as one of the spiritual barons in the country, and his brother Benedictines, obviously lived in luxury.

The Abbot's scattered flocks amounted to 13,400 sheep, and several of his manors each rendered two hundred pigs annually, whilst the manor of Doddington kept a stock of 100 dairy cows, and appears to have been an important vaccary supplying butter and cheese to the monastery.

Grain which grew in abundance on the Abbot's marshland manors, was taken to and stored in the monastery's large barn in readiness for grinding into flour for the bakery; whereas the beehives in Methwold and Histon rendered an annual supply of honey and wax.

Whatever the considerable number of manors governed by the Ely monastery could not supply was bought elsewhere, as it became immensely rich. Its wool crop alone yielded a vast fortune.

RIVAL MARKETS

The grant to hold a market in a town was a privilege granted by the King, although he generally delegated the right to a baron or a spiritual lord.

Markets were an important source of income for a town, as apart from making a profit on rents charged for having a stall, tolls were often levied on goods brought in by outsiders.

The Great Survey lists nine towns in Suffolk which had markets, one of which was the ancient village of Hoxne in the Waveney Valley, which claimed to be the place where the martyrdom of St. Edmund occurred. The manor of Hoxne formed part of the estates governed by the Bishop of East Anglia, who had his chief Suffolk seat there.

The small agricultural settlement of Eye lay about four miles south of Hoxne. It was given by the Conqueror to William Malet, one of his most loyal supporters. Malet also received 201 manors in Suffolk as well as lands in Norfolk and Lincolnshire. He was made Sheriff of Suffolk and chose the growing town of Eye as the chief seat of his lordship.He was granted permission by the King to erect a large castle in the centre of the town, and established a market in the outer bailey of the castle. By holding it on Saturdays, he earned the displeasure of the bishop, as the market at Hoxne was held on the same day of the week, and the bishop saw it as direct competition.

William Malet died during the siege of Ely in 1071, and his son, Robert, inherited his estates and also his position as Sheriff of Suffolk. He continued to hold the market his father had established at Eye on Saturdays, which became very popular and brought prosperity to the thriving town.

Thetford Castle, with the highest motte in England, was built for Roger Bigod, the Warrior from Calvados. – EARLY TWENTIETH CENTURY POSTCARD.

But the growing prosperity and popularity of the market at Eye was to the detriment of rival Hoxne, whose market became of low interest and 'little worth'. Eventually the bishop decided to change Hoxne's market day to Friday in an attempt to attract business back to Hoxne, but to no avail.

The market at Eye continued to flourish, whereas the one held at Hoxne continued to decline.

DUNWICH-BY-THE-SEA

The most important manor held by Robert Malet was the town of Dunwich, on the Suffolk coast, in the Hundred of Blything.

Since the Conquest, Dunwich had grown and had become very prosperous. At the time of the Great Survey, it was listed as a considerable and important town, having a population of about 3,000, three churches, and a port with a fleet of fishing boats returning 68,000 herrings annually. It ranked amongst the ten most prominent towns in England.

But the Survey also mentions the coastal erosion that would one day bring about the town's demise. In the twenty years following the Conquest 240 acres of land had been reclaimed by the sea, and every year the North Sea storms eroded a little more, narrowing the distance between the town and the coast.

THE WARRIOR FROM CALVADOS

Roger Bigod was a minor noble from the Calvados region of Normandy. He came to England with the Conqueror and, for his valour and support at the Battle of Hastings, was rewarded with 100 estates in Suffolk and 6 in Essex.

Bigod served his royal master well and acted as one of the King's close advisers. He was given responsibility for the defence of the Suffolk coast, and when King Sweyn of Denmark sailed up the River Orwell with a raiding party in 1069, he again proved his worth by defeating the Danes in battle near Ipswich.

In recognition of his achievement he was further rewarded with several lands that had previously belonged to the deposed Saxon Bishop Athelmaer.

When the Earl of Norfolk rebelled against the King in 1071, Bigod's military skills were once again called upon to assist in quelling the uprising.

The fall and disgrace of Earl Ralph led to Bigod acquiring the majority of his Norfolk lands, being appointed constable of Norwich Castle, as well as becoming a Royal Justice.

In the year of the Great Survey, Bigod was listed as one of the chief landowners in East Anglia. He was a Steward of the Royal Household who often attended the King and, by his influence at court, obtained the Sheriffdom of Norfolk.

From his stronghold at Norwich the fearsome warrior toured the county dispensing the King's justice and gathering the royal taxes.

CHAPTER THREE

The Norman Settlement, 1087-1133

DEATH OF THE CONQUEROR

The year 1087 was 'a very heavy and pestiferous year' according to the old chroniclers. They recorded that a feverish illness spread throughout the land with such severity that 50% of the people were affected, and many died.

When the fever began to subside, there were fierce storms accompanied by thunder and lightning, followed by famine throughout the land 'so that many died wretched deaths'. While his subjects in England were suffering, the Conqueror was on the Continent fighting a war with his old adversary, King Philip of France. He was laying waste to the countryside around the town of Mantes, when his horse slipped as he urged it to leap over a ditch.

King William was thrown forward on to the pommel of the saddle. In severe pain, he was carried back to Rouen, where it was discovered he had suffered an acute internal rupture. He lingered in agony for several days, but eventually died on the 9th September 1087.

Before his death William had instructed that his eldest son, Robert should succeed to the Dukedom of Normandy , and that his youngest son, Henry, should receive £5,000, but he did not name his successor to the throne of England, as the old Saxon kingship had been elective.

However, he made his preference clear in a message he sent to Archbishop Lanfranc by expressing the wish that his second son, William Rufus, should have possession of the Kingdom.

Upon hearing the news of his father's death, Rufus lost no time in crossing the Channel and hurrying to London to claim the throne. He was immediately acknowledged as his father's successor, and was crowned King in Westminster Abbey by Archbishop Lanfranc on 28th September 1087.

REBELLION

The new King, William II, was more commonly known as Rufus because of his ruddy complexion. He was vain, greedy, arrogant, blasphemous, and unpopular with the barons.

Most of the barons, who possessed lands on both sides of the Channel, found they now had to pay homage to two masters following the division of Normandy and England. They would have preferred the easy-going Duke Robert to have been crowned King of England.

As the eldest son, Duke Robert thought it his birth-right to have succeeded his father as king, and disputed the succession of his brother to the English throne. His militant uncle Odo, Bishop of Bayeux and Earl of Kent, was only too keen to support him, and instigated a rebellion in 1088.

The Bishop-Earl was a substantial landowner in East Anglia, holding 44 manors in Essex, several in Suffolk, and the Lordship of Rising and Snettisham in Norfolk.

Annoyed by the separation of Normandy and England, and encouraged by Odo's stand against Rufus, several other barons declared their support for Duke Robert.

Roger Bigod, Sheriff of Norfolk, for instance, whose family had strong ties with the Bayeux region of Normandy, garrisoned Norwich Castle and plundered the surrounding countryside. On one foray he attacked and sacked Cambridge, conveying the spoils back to Norwich.

Robert Malet, Baron of Eye, and Richard FitzGilbert, of Clare, who was related to Bishop Odo, both put their castles on a war footing, but did little else to support Odo's rebellion. In fact the majority of the East Anglian barons did nothing more than fortify their castles in what seems to have been a half-hearted attempt to support Odo in his rebellion against Rufus.

A MORTAL WOUND

Rufus had no difficulty in raising a formidable army from the English populace, who were easily won over by the promise of tax relief and a fairer government. William de Warenne, Lord of Acre, came out of seclusion to fight for Rufus, and was made Earl of Surrey for his loyalty.

Rebels in the west and midlands were quickly defeated, but Bishop Odo and his brother, the Count of Mortain, stubbornly held out in Pevensey Castle on the Sussex coast.

Rufus and his army laid siege to the castle for six weeks, during which time William de Warenne was seriously wounded in the leg by an arrow and taken to the Priory of Lewes. Pevensey Castle was completely cut off, and the two rebel leaders were forced to surrender owing to a shortage of food. But William de Warenne died from the effects of his wound on 24th June. He was buried in the church of Lewes Priory next to his beloved wife, Lady Gundrada. His eldest son, also named William, succeeded to his titles and estates.

A NEW LORD FOR RISING

Rufus was surprisingly lenient with the majority of the rebel barons, although both Robert Malet and Richard FitzGilbert remained out of favour. FitzGilbert decided to retire to a monastery, where he spent the rest of his life, leaving his estates in the hands of his son Gilbert FitzRichard. But the Clare family never found much favour at the court of Rufus.

The wily old warrior, Roger Bigod, lost his position of Sheriff of Norfolk, and was replaced by Humphrey the Chamberlain. However, he somehow wormed his way back into favour and retained his position as Steward of the Royal Household. He remained loyal to Rufus throughout the monarch's reign.

Rufus, however, could not forgive his uncle, Bishop Odo, for his part in plotting a rebellion against him. He confiscated all his English lands, and banished him from England forever.

His Norfolk lands and titles, which included the Lordship of Rising and Snettisham, were given to William de Albini, with the authority to claim a half-share of the customs, taxes and tolls collected in the port of Lynn.

William de Albini came to England after Rufus had been crowned King. The son of the Lord of St. Martin d'Aubigny in Normandy, he backed Rufus during the Bishop of Bayeux's rebellion.

He was also appointed Lord of Buckenham in Norfolk, where he built a large castle, which became the centre of his Norfolk estates, which collectively became known as the Honour of Buckenham. He supported Rufus throughout his reign, and consequently prospered.

RICHES AND RELICS

The Fenland Island of the Ram, more commonly known as Ramsey, was once described as the 'fairest of the fenny islands'.

Previously isolated by 'deep and boggy quagmires', its status was enhanced by the foundation of Ramsey Abbey during the reign of King Edgar.

A stone and gravel causeway was constructed for easier access to the uplands, and its terrain was converted to tillage. The island thus became plentiful in wheat, 'fair gardens, fat pastures, and rich meadows'.

The Abbey of Ramsey, supported by generous benefactors, thus became rich and powerful, acquiring vast estates in the counties of Northamptonshire, Bedfordshire, Hertfordshire, Suffolk, Norfolk, Cambridgeshire and Huntingdonshire.

It also became well-known for its valuable collection of relics, which included the bones of St. Felix, Apostle of East Anglia, the bones of Ethelbert and Ethelred, two Kentish princes, the jawbone of St. Egwin, the cowl of St.

Alphege, and the much prized body of St. Ivo, a Persian Archbishop.

In the first year of the reign of Rufus, the abbacy fell vacant with the death of the Saxon Abbot Ailsi, said to have been 'a man of prudence and industry', whose only notable deed was the rather dubious claim that he was the instigator of the Feast of the Immaculate Conception.

Rufus chose to replace Ailsi with a Norman monk, Herbert de Losinga, from the Abbey of Fecamp, and appointed him Abbot of Ramsey.

A distinguished scholar, educated at Fecamp, Herbert eventually rose to become Prior of the monastery, but was disdainfully referred to as 'a monk, born of a monk', although there is no evidence to suggest that his father was in holy orders when Herbert was born.

He is said to have ruled the Abbey of Ramsey with 'skill and wisdom', introducing many customs from the Abbey of Fecamp. Being accustomed to French cuisine, he also brought over French cooks to impart their culinary skills to their English counterparts at Ramsey.

Although he enjoyed the favour of King William Rufus by serving the royal household as a steward, and as a chaplain, Herbert was ambitious, and aimed to use his position to gain even higher office.

A CASE OF SIMONY

From the early days of his reign, it was inevitable that the extravagance of Rufus would lead him into financial problems. He had spent a fortune bribing the populace to support him against the rebellion of Bishop Odo, whilst continuing to live in luxury at court and indulge in his love of finery.

The rapid depletion of the treasury, bequeathed to him by his father, prompted him to double taxes which made him even more unpopular with the people. He also appointed Ranulf Flambard as his chief chaplain, whose true assignment was to raise more money for his royal master.

Flambard was a man of fiery temperament, as his name implies, and was said to be utterly unscrupulous. One chronicler described him as 'a torch of iniquity'.

He devised a legal means of raising money for the King by deliberately keeping abbacies and bishoprics vacant so that the revenues from their estates could be paid into the Exchequer. The longer vacancies were prolonged, the more revenues poured into the King's hands.

When an appointment was made to a vacant position, it was given to the King's preferred nominee, who was expected to make a substantial payment to him for the privilege.

Herbert de Losinga had ruled the Abbey of Ramsey for three years when the bishopric of Thetford fell vacant following the death of Bishop William Beaufeu in 1091.

Seeing the opportunity for promotion, ambitious Herbert secured the bishopric by paying the sum of £1,000 to Flambard, with the eager consent of Rufus, and was duly appointed Bishop of Thetford.

EUDO THE CONSTABLE

The de Rye family came from the Bessin region of Normandy, taking their name from the town of Ryes, which lay a distance of three leagues from Bayeux.

Eudo de Rye, the youngest son of Hubert, lord of Ryes, became a personal attendant to the Duke of Normandy, accompanying the Duke to England with the invading force.

He was well-rewarded, for serving the Conqueror faithfully, with 26 manors in Essex and large holdings in Cambridgeshire, Bedfordshire, Hertfordshire and Norfolk, in addition to being made a steward of the royal household.

Eudo was present at the Conqueror's death in Rouen, and followed his master's wish by supporting the succession of Rufus to the throne.

The county of Essex formed part of the diocese of London, and the town and Castle of Colchester were in the charge of the Bishop of London who had installed his underling, Walchelin, as custodian.

Walchelin soon became unpopular by imposing extortionate and excessive tax demands, confiscating land and property from those who could not pay, and other 'outlawries'.

His tyranny eventually aroused the burgesses of Colchester to complain to the King, and request that Walchelin be replaced by the more toadish Eudo de Rye.

Surprisingly, the King complied with their request, and appointed Eudo constable of the royal town and castle of Colchester.

The people of Colchester became more satisfied under Eudo's rule, but his tenure was uneventful, apart from improving the fortifications of the castle and strengthening the town's wall.

THE VOW OF PICOT'S WIFE

The change of monarch brought little respite to the people of Cambridgeshire from the ruthless Picot, as Rufus confirmed his position as Sheriff of the County. 'The Prowling Wolf' continued his reign of terror, for the passing years had not diminished his greed.

But in 1092, his wife, Hugolina, was suddenly taken dangerously ill. The King's physicians and other prominent medical men were called to attend her, but they all agreed that nothing could be done to save her.

Hugolina, fearing that her imminent death was divine retribution for her husband's misdeeds, vowed to God and St. Giles, her patron saint, that if they helped her recover, she would establish a religious house and dedicate it to St. Giles.

The reason why Hugolina devoted herself to St. Giles is unknown. He was an Athenian by birth, who lived in the seventh century, and was revered for his extraordinary piety.

Whatever the reason, her faith in God and St. Giles confounded the medics, only three days after making her vow she made a miraculous recovery.

Picot was compelled to fulfil his wife's vow, and spent a fortune establishing and endowing a religious house dedicated to St. Giles, near Cambridge Castle, with apartments for six Augustinian canons, after first seeking permission from the Bishop of Lincoln in whose diocese Cambridgeshire was situated.

He richly endowed the Priory with lands and churches from his barony, a gesture which cost him much of the fortune he had accumulated pitilessly from the people of Cambridgeshire.

But neither he nor his wife lived to see their foundation flourish, for they both died within two years after the foundation stone was laid. Their son, Robert, succeeded to the barony.

FLAMBARD AT ELY

Progression in building the new church at Ely had been very slow, mainly because of the laxitude and neglect of those whom Abbot Simeon had committed to the task in 1083, and remained unfinished at the time of his death on 20th November 1093.

He was 100 years of age when he died, and had governed the abbey for twelve years. His body was laid in the old church to await burial. The monks who had accompanied him from Winchester were instructed to keep watch over his body and pray for his soul, but unfortunately, they had other notions.

Casting aside any respect for their dead Abbot, they decided to rob the abbey of whatever valuables they could lay their hands on, then fled to Winchester with their spoils.

They stopped at an inn in Guildford, intending to rest for the night, but fell to heavy drinking and continued imbibing until they could hardly stand.

When they eventually retired, one of the monks carelessly knocked over a lighted candle, resulting in the building being burnt down.

All the monks escaped, but their plunder was lost in the fire, and they eventually arrived at their monastery in Winchester empty handed.

Receiving news of the death of Abbot Simeon, Rufus lost no time in sending his infamous minister, Ranulf Flambard, to Ely to take possession of the abbeys temporalities.

As soon as Abbot Simeon was buried, Flambard summoned the remaining seventy-two monks to a meeting and made an inventory of everything the abbey owned. After consulting with them at length, he agreed to allow them £70 a year for clothing and £60 a year for food.

Additionally, they were allowed 200 pigs from their estates, all butter and cheese from the vaccaries, ten measures of wheat and ten measures of malt weekly, and a quantity of wine for use on Saturdays and Feast days. All other income was to go to the King's treasury.

Although the monks income had been severely reduced they still lived in comparative comfort compared to the poor peasants of the region, but the main beneficiary was Rufus. He kept the Abbacy of Ely vacant for seven years after Simeon's death, whilst the monastery's revenues poured into his treasury.

THE SHRINE OF ST. EDMUND

Abbot Baldwin had held his position in Bury St. Edmunds monastery for thirty years and must have often wondered as he grew older if he would live to see the new church, the building of which he had begun several years earlier, completed and used.

But the advancing years did not deprive him of the satisfaction of attending the consecration ceremony of the finished church on 29th. April 1095.

It was considered one of the largest and grandest churches in England, and was consecrated in a ceremony conducted by Walkelin, Bishop of Winchester. The body of St. Edmund was transferred to its hallowed resting place, a splendid tomb and shrine, directly behind the high altar.

Ranulf Flambard was among the many important prelates and nobles who attended the ceremony, but was more interested in assessing the wealth of the monastery than the transfer of a revered corpse to its new resting place in the newly built church.

Bury Abbey was the richest in England, and the King was interested in its vast revenues. Flambard must have noted the frailty of old Abbot Baldwin during the ceremony, but the greedy King had to wait two more years before Baldwin passed away.

Following his death, Flambard took over the temporalities of the abbey, and kept the abbacy vacant while he pillaged its great wealth for the further enrichment of his royal master.

BANISHMENT OF PICOT'S SON

Several barons grew tired of the King's tyranny and oppressive taxes, and formed a plot to replace him with his cousin Stephen, Earl of Albemarle.

A large army was assembled from all over England under the leadership of

Robert de Mowbray, Earl of Northumberland, and prepared for confrontation with the King in the north-east.

But few of the barons involved in the earlier rebellion were keen to join in, and Robert Picot, Lord of Bourn, son of the late infamous Sheriff of Cambridgeshire, appears to have been the only baron from East Anglia who participated in the uprising.

As soon as the disturbance began, Rufus acted promptly and marched north with a strong army, which quickly laid siege to Robert de Mowbray's castles and easily defeated the Earl and his rebels.

This time Rufus dealt severely with those who had plotted against him. Robert de Mowbray was imprisoned and many others were put to death. Robert Picot managed to escape the King's clutches by fleeing to Normandy, but Rufus was determined to punish him.

He banished Picot from England and confiscated his Lordship of Bourn, which he held for the rest of his reign, as yet another source of income to replenish his ever-empty purse.

A REPENTANT SINNER

Herbert de Losinga had struggled with his conscience for two years since he had been appointed Bishop of Thetford. The fact that he had obtained the See by simony, which was a sin according to the law of the church, played heavily on his mind.

In 1093 his conscience finally got the better of him, and he decided to journey to Rome to seek absolution from the Pope.

He eventually crossed the Alps, after making an arduous six-week journey through Europe in the summer of 1093, only to find Italy in turmoil, with a power struggle between two rival Pontiffs, namely Pope Urban II and Pope Clement III. Undeterred, Herbert travelled on to Rome, and was relieved when he arrived to find that Urban II had regained control of the city from his rival.

Herbert willingly confessed his sin to the French Pope Urban, who, like himself, had been a former monk. He surrendered his ring and staff to the Pope, who absolved him and immediately restored him to office, but imposed a penance upon him.

This consisted of the task of erecting churches and religious houses in his diocese, but he also gained permission from the Pope to transfer the seat of his bishopric from Thetford to Norwich, and began to organise the building of churches and monasteries in East Anglia with zeal when he returned from Rome.

Herbert founded the parish church of St. Margaret, and the Priory church of St. Mary Magdalen at King's Lynn. which he endowed with lands in the area.

He also established the church of St. Nicholas at Great Yarmouth as well as the priory of St. Leonard, which he had founded in Norwich.

The Church of St. Nicholas, the patron saint of fishermen, was one of the largest parish churches in England, covering an area of 23,000 square feet. During its monastic period it contained 17 chapels, used by the sixteen guilds of the town.

On 9th April 1094, Herbert officially transferred the See of East Anglia from Thetford to Norwich, where he decided to erect a new cathedral on a suitable site in a meadow, called 'Cowholme', close to the River Wensum.

He persuaded several nobles, including Roger Bigod, to support his project, and obtained substantial grants from them. The building of the cathedral commenced in 1096, and Herbert de Losinga laid the foundation stone himself.

A VERY GREAT STIR

According to the Anglo-Saxon Chronicle, in 1095 'there was a very great stir through all the nation'. Both the English and the Normans were stirred into an adventure, the like of which had never been seen before.

It was caused when the Holy Land, which had formed part of the Christian Byzantine Empire for centuries, fell to the infidel Turks in 1075, who continued their conquests by invading Asia Minor, imposing a serious threat to the city of Constantinople.

The Emperor Alexius, anxious to halt the advance of the Turks, appealed to Pope Urban for help, who responded by crossing the Alps to his native France to rally support for the beleaguered Empire.

At the Synod of Clermont, held on 27th November 1095, he proclaimed a Crusade to free the Holy places from the Turks.

Several princes rallied to his call, including Robert , Duke of Normandy, who, in order to pay for raising his army, was obliged to mortgage his duchy to his brother, King William Rufus, for the sum of 10,000 marks.

The extravagant Rufus had exhausted his treasury, and in order to pay the lump sum to his brother was forced to raise the money by imposing a severe tax on the whole of England.

His trusty minister, Flambard, who had exploited every device he could think of to extract more money from the people to replenish his master's treasury, consequently imposed a second Danegeld, thus doubling the ordinary rate of tax, not only on laymen but also on the church.

Bishops and abbots were forced to strip shrines and altars of all gold and silver ornaments and crosses, precious gospel-books and vestments, and the barons complained bitterly as Flambard drained every penny possible from them.

In spite of complaints, the money was raised and shipped across the Channel by September 1096, thus enabling Duke Robert to form an army of about 15,000 men, comprised of Normans, English and Bretons, all united in a common cause.

In October they set off on the long trek to the Holy Land. Among the English contingent were William Percy, a Northern Baron, Edgar the Athling, and from East Anglia, Aubrey de Vere, Lord of Hedingham.

Odo, the Bishop of Bayeux, as ambitious and adventurous as ever, joined his nephew's crusade, but was taken seriously ill in Italy, where he died.

THE STAR OF THE DE VERES

By the end of April 1097 the crusaders had crossed the Bosphorus, and marched south through Anatolia and arrived in Syria in October, where they encamped outside the important city of Antioch.

It was vital that the Crusaders captured Antioch before they could continue their march, but the city walls were well-defended, so they had no option but to lay siege to it.

The siege lasted for seven months, and many fierce skirmishes took place between the two sides. During one of the skirmishes with the Turks the Crusaders fell into confusion after darkness had fallen. When all seemed lost, a brilliant five pointed star is said to have appeared on the shield of Aubrey de Vere, which illuminated the whole battlefield and inspired the Crusaders to re-form and win a resounding victory over the Turks.

From that day, the de Vere family incorporated a white five-pointed star in the top left-hand quarter of their coat of arms.

Following de Vere's 'miracle' defeat of the Turks at Antioch, the city fell to the Crusaders in April 1098, and they marched on to Jerusalem, which was captured, after a long siege, on 15th. April 1099.

Robert of Normandy was one who played a leading role in all of these events. Chroniclers record stories of him slicing Turks in half with a single blow of his sword.

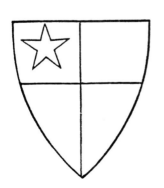

The Star of the de Vere's, depicted on their coat of arms.

The stories may have been exaggerated, but there is no doubt that he was an outstanding soldier. Having played a major part in the capture of Jerusalem, Robert of Normandy returned home to reclaim his duchy from Rufus.

Aubrey de Vere also returned home,

but was so uplifted by his illuminating experience on the battlefield that he went into seclusion as a monk at Colne Priory, where he remained until his death in 1112.

THE WRETCHED BOROUGH

During the long rule of Turold of Fecamp over the Monastery of Peterborough, the abbey and town became so impoverished that it became known as 'The Wretched Borough'.

Turold plundered the abbey's wealth for his personal enrichment, gave away its lands to his relatives, and spent more by building a castle, which became known as Turold's Mount.

There he thought he could live in safety, protected by an army of knights, upon whom he lavished lands and money to secure their loyalty. Ambitious to gain promotion in the church, he became impatient when nothing came of his efforts, so embezzled more of Peterborough Abbey's resources to procure the bishopric of Beavais in Normandy.

Having purchased the bishopric, he travelled to Beavais, where he expected he would be welcomed as bishop, but his stay only lasted three days. The monks of Beavais detested him and made his stay so uncomfortable that he was driven out.

He returned to England and paid Rufus a substantial sum of money to be reinstated as Abbot of Peterborough, but it is said that he 'neither loved his monastery, nor his convent'.

The monks of the abbey were no doubt relieved when he died in 1098, having ruled over them for 28 years, his only notable achievement being to have squandered two thirds of the abbey's wealth.

When news of Turold's death reached Rufus, he sent his obnoxious minister Ranulf Flambard to seize what was left of its temporalities, and the abbacy remained vacant until after the death of Rufus.

ACCIDENT OR ASSASSINATION?

Like his father, King William, Rufus enjoyed the thrill of the hunt. In the month of August, which was the fat season for red deer, he would spend as much time as possible with the hunt.

In the summer of 1100, Rufus and several companions took up residence at the royal hunting lodge at Brokenhurst in the New Forest. Among those present were his brother Prince Henry, and a contingent of barons from East Anglia, including Gilbert FitzRichard of Clare, Roger Bigod, Robert Malet of Eye, Eudo de Rye, and Walter Tirel. After enjoying a sumptuous lunch on Thursday 2nd August, the hunting party set off, but dispersed and took up positions at a clearing to await their prey.

Accident or assassination? The death of King William Rufus in the New Forest.

When the first stag appeared in the clearing Walter Tirel immediately let fly an arrow which missed the stag and struck the King in the chest. Mortally wounded, Rufus fell from his horse and died shortly after.

The hunting party panicked and took flight, leaving the dead king in the forest. The barons hastened to fortify their castles and Walter Tirel fled to the coast and boarded a ship bound for Normandy.

Prince Henry first hurried to Winchester to secure the treasury, and thence to London to press his claim to the throne. Three days after the death of Rufus he was crowned King of England in Westminster Abbey.

In the meantime, some servants were detailed to convey the body of the detested King to Winchester, ironically on the very cart that was meant to transport the dead stags shot during the hunt.

Rufus was unceremoniously buried beneath the tower of Winchester Cathedral. Mass was not said and the bells remained silent at the tyrants funeral service.

According to a chronicler, King Rufus was 'hateful both to God and to people'. Seven years after he was buried the tower of the cathedral collapsed, and was said to be a protest from heaven against the interment of such an evil man in so sacred a place.

But the death of Rufus was widely believed to be the result of a conspiracy, hatched between Prince Henry and some of the East Anglian barons, who wished to rid the country of such an oppressive ruler.

Tirel, who had fired the first misdirected arrow at the stag against the usual custom of allowing the King the privilege, was the steward of the estates of Gilbert de Clare, who was a close friend of Prince Henry. Tirel was never accused of murder and adamantly denied the fact that he was the one who fired the arrow. Whether the death of Rufus was accidental, or the result of a pre-planned plot to kill him, remains a mystery that can never be solved.

A HAUGHTY ABBOT

To placate his subjects, new King Henry arrested his brother's hated minister, Ranulf Flambard, and cast him into the Tower of London, from which he made a rare escape, no doubt with some assistance. He then fled across the Channel to seek refuge at the court of Duke Robert.

King Henry also issued a Charter of Liberties, which included a grant to 'God's Holy Church', to annul the 'evil customs by which the kingdom had been oppressed'. He then set about filling the abbacies which had deliberately been kept vacant by the late king.

He appointed Robert, an illegitimate son of the Earl of Chester, as Abbot of Bury St. Edmunds, and Richard de Clare, the brother of Gilbert FitzRichard, Baron of Clare, to fill the vacant position at Ely.

Richard de Clare had been brought up from infancy in the monastery of Bec in Normandy, and was acclaimed for his learning of philosophy and divinity. He threw himself wholeheartedly into the building of the new church which his predecessor had begun. But in 1102 he fell foul of several dignitaries when he was summoned to a council meeting of bishops, abbots and barons at Westminster, to discuss several new constitutions relating to ecclesiastical discipline.

Richard arrived at the meeting with such blatant pomp and ceremony that several barons who were hostile to the increasing power and wealth of the de Clare family decided to clip their wings by bringing Richard to trial, claiming that his haughty manner was an insult to the King and that he did not show due honour and respect to his sovereign.

The special court held to judge complaints against Richard found him guilty, and ordered him to surrender his Pastoral Staff, thus deposing him of his abbacy.

But Richard did not accept the decision of the court and refused to give up his emblem of office. The King, reluctant to become involved in the dispute, ordered Anselm, Archbishop of Canterbury, to settle it, even if it meant taking the matter to Rome.

Anselm was also unwilling to give judgement, so reluctantly set off for Rome with Richard in 1103. After hearing the case Pope Pascal reversed the sentence of the court and issued a Bull restoring Richard to his abbacy.

On his return to England, Richard met with favour and goodwill from King Henry, and was joyfully welcomed back to the Abbey of Ely by the monks.

NORWICH CATHEDRAL

The construction of Norwich Cathedral was perhaps the greatest building project ever undertaken in Norfolk, but progress was too slow for the satisfaction of Bishop Herbert de Losinga.

The labour force was enormous and not entirely made up of volunteers. To inspire everyone involved to work harder, he issued a written admonition which read: 'Pluck up heart once more; lift up the hands that hang down and strengthen the feeble knees. Persist untiringly in your work, let not your hand and foot rest'.

Bishop de Losinga seems to have had little or no concern for the welfare of the serfs who had been compelled to work on the building. He expressed his view by writing; 'The master is served by the compliance of his slaves, and the compliance of his slaves cannot be secured without the lash'.

According to a local tradition the Saxon serfs and the Norman workers were divided into teams, each team working on a different side of the building to prevent conflict.

The cost of the building, was partly raised from Herbert's own purse, and partly by contributions gathered from people of the diocese by monks, whom Herbert had specially trained to stimulate people into parting with their money.

The plan of the building was based on that of the church of the monastery of Fecamp, and it is likely that Herbert followed the Norman custom of building from the east end and working westwards.

The cathedral itself was mainly constructed of flint and rubble, faced with stone brought from Caen in Normandy. This was shipped from the continent in galleys which sailed up the River Wensum and thence along a specially constructed canal so that the stones could be deposited as near as possible to the building site.

After five years of toil, the presbytery, transepts, choir, and the lower part of the tower were completed. At a ceremony held on the 26th September 1101, the building was formally consecrated and dedicated to the Holy and Undivided Trinity.

THE HANDSOME EARL

Having succeeded to his father's vast possessions in 1088, William de Warenne, 2nd Earl of Surrey, remained on favourable terms with King William Rufus by keeping clear of political intrigues and concentrating on the development of his estates.

He improved his late father's fortified house at Acre, and patronised the religious house of Clunaic monks by moving them to a more spacious site south of the castle, where he granted them orchards, and all the cultivated land between the site of the priory and the castle.

In 1093 the handsome bachelor Earl decided it was about time he married, and set his eyes upon Edith, daughter of King Malcolm III of Scotland. At the time Edith was in a convent at Romsey, where she was completing her education under the guidance of her Aunt Christina, a nun.

Edith, who had been compelled to wear a black veil by her Aunt throughout her studies, was said to be beautiful and Earl William paid suit to her, constantly proposing marriage.

But Edith declined his proposals, saying that she was firmly devoted to religious life. Apparently it was merely an excuse to decline marriage to the Earl, for chronicles record that the real reason she did so was because 'she was reserved for higher destiny', and was already betrothed to marry a Prince of the Royal House of England.

Three months after Prince Henry had been crowned King in Westminster Abbey, the marriage of Edith, who adopted the name of Matilda, and King Henry took place.

William de Warenne was outraged and bore animosity towards King Henry for stealing the hand of Edith from him, and seized every opportunity to mock and deride the King by calling him names, such as 'Deer's Foot,' because Henry, like his father, loved hunting, and in his youth often pursued the deer on foot because he could not afford a horse.

In 1101, King Henry dispossessed William of his title and lands after he had supported Duke Robert's claim to the English throne. William fled to Normandy, and two years later was one of the exiled nobles who persuaded Duke Robert to invade England.

The Duke and his army landed at Portsmouth, and several English barons, including Robert Malet, Lord of Eye, rallied to his cause.

But when it came to actually fighting against his brother, Duke Robert decided that it would be best to resolve the matter peacefully, and gave up his claim to the throne on payment of 3,000 marks.

Soon afterwards, William de Warenne's title and estates were restored to him, mainly due to the insistence of Duke Robert, William having overcome his animosity towards the King for marrying Edith. From then on he became a faithful and trusted friend to King Henry and his Queen. Robert Malet was less fortunate. The King confiscated all his lands and estates and banished him from England. The King gave the castle and Honour of Eye to his nephew, Stephen of Blois.

William de Warenne eventually fell in love with Isobel, the wife of the Earl of Leicester, and for some time they had a secret affair until they eloped and married bigamously before the death of Isobel's husband.

The Earl of Leicester paid little attention to the indiscretions and loss of his wife, and made no attempt to recover her. William and Isobel lived happily together, producing a family of three sons and two daughters.

TRANSLATION OF ST. ETHELDREDA

Restored to his position of Abbot of the monastery of Ely, Richard de Clare gave his undivided attention to resuming the building of the new church, having the ambition to see it completed during his lifetime.

By 1106 the building was advanced enough for Richard to transfer the remains of St. Etheldreda, St. Sexburga, St. Ermenilda, and St. Withburga from the old church.

Invitations were duly sent to the Archbishop of Canterbury and other church dignitaries to attend the re-interment ceremony, but the Archbishop, and many others, declined the invitations and made excuses, probably because they disliked Richard's haughty and superior manner.

Among those who did attend the solemn ceremony, which took place on 17th October 1106, was Herbert de Losinga, Bishop of Norwich, Aldwin,

Bishop de Losinga induced his labour force to work harder by the use of the lash.

Abbot of Ramsey, Richard, Abbot of St. Albans, Gunter, Abbot of Thorney, Wido, Abbot of Pershore, and Nicholas, Archdeacon of Lincoln.

They all followed in procession behind the marble coffin containing the body of St. Etheldreda as it was carried into the new church, and stood in silence as it was re-interred in front of the high altar.

After hymns had been sung and prayers said, Bishop Herbert gave a lengthy discourse on the life, death and miracles of St. Etheldreda. When he finally finished, the coffins containing the remains of the other Saints were brought into the new church and re-interred near the coffin of St. Etheldreda.

The old church, which was situated near the new one, was then demolished, allowing for the improvement and enlargement of the domestic buildings of the monastery. Abbot Richard was well-pleased to see his ambition nearing fulfilment.

THE KING'S BUTLER

William de Albini, who had been given the Lordships of Rising, Snettisham and Buckenham by Rufus, was also appointed to the office of Chief Butler to the King.

The position gave him responsibility of 'Keeper of the Butts', which entailed looking after the wine, stored in butts in the cellar, or buttery, and to provide the King with adequate drink.

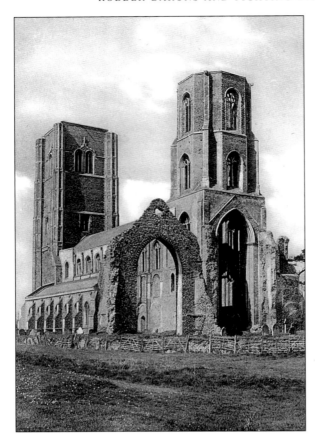

The Priory of Wymondham was founded by William de Albini, as a burial place for himself and his descendants. – EARLY TWENTIETH CENTURY POSTCARD.

William, who held the position under Rufus and his successor Henry I, had charge of a large workforce, consisting of ushers, cellarmen, coopers, cup-bearers and labourers.

He also had to engage carters, carts and horses, as the King's court was often on the move. The buttery therefore had to be mobile to supply the King, wherever he went, with an adequate supply of his favourite tipple.

When William was not attending to his special duties of butler to the King, he lived at his castle at Old Buckenham from where he ran his vast Norfolk estates, no doubt ably assisted by his wife, Maud, considering his frequent absences. Maud was the daughter of Roger Bigod.

One of William's manors in Norfolk was Wymondham, which had been given to him by Rufus for his services as Chief Butler.

Wymondham, which derives its name from the Saxon Win Monte Ham, meaning 'the pleasant village on a mount', was a prosperous little town which had been granted authority to hold a market on Fridays by King Henry.

The market proved very popular and was a major reason why William decided to found a Priory in Wymondham in 1107. The Priory was built for a prior and twelve monks of the Order of St. Benedict, as a dependency of the Abbey of St. Albans, where William's uncle, Richard de Albini was Abbot.

The Priory church also served as the town's parochial church, shared by the monks and people of Wymondham. William endowed his foundation with large estates, including one third of the manor of Wymondham.

King Henry also endowed the Priory with lands, and the privilege of claiming the numerous wrecks off the Norfolk coast between Eccles, Happisburgh and Tunstead, as well as a annual supply of 2,000 eels from the village of Hilgay.

But the main reason for William founding the Priory was for the purpose of a burial place for himself and his descendants, and that the chief duty of the monks was to offer continual prayers for the souls of him and his family.

ROGER BIGOD'S BODY

As the years advanced, the old warrior Roger Bigod reflected on his misdeeds and concluded that he had not lived an honest and honourable life. Fearing that the gates of heaven might be closed to him, he formed the idea of going on a pilgrimage to Jerusalem to atone for his sins. His steward wisely dissuaded him from undertaking such a dangerous journey at his time of life, and suggested that he might consider establishing a religious house as an acceptable and more practical alternative.

Bigod, persuaded by his steward, chose the abandoned cathedral church at Thetford for situating his new priory, and applied to the Abbot of Cluny in France to send twelve monks to assist him in its restoration.

The Abbot replied that he could not spare any monks from Cluny, but said that he would send twelve monks from the Cluniac Priory of Lewes in Sussex, as well as Malgod, who was to serve as Prior.

For three years the seconded monks and their helpers laboured to adapt the site into a suitable priory, but the site eventually proved too small and the surrounding buildings in the town did not allow room for enlargement.

In 1107, Malgod's successor, Prior Stephen, suggested that Bigod move the priory to spacious land at the side of the Little Ouse river, and with the sanction of the King, Bigod agreed.

Shortly afterwards, Bishop Herbert de Losinga broke the first sod on the site with his own hands, and King Henry, who was staying at his palace in Thetford, laid the foundation stone. Eight days after the ceremony, Roger

The remains of St Mary's Priory, Thetford, the intended burial place of Roger Bigod.

Bigod died, and was temporarily buried in the old cathedral church until the new Priory church was completed.

When Bishop de Losinga heard of Bigod's death, he was determined that he should be buried in Norwich Cathedral, and sent a party of monks to Thetford to dig up and carry Bigod's body to Norwich.

Bigod's widow, Lady Alice, and Prior Stephen, protested strongly to the bishop over his high-handed action, and implored him to return Bigod's body to Thetford so that it could be interred in the Priory Church in accordance with his wishes.

Bishop de Losinga ignored their pleas, inciting Prior Stephen to send several monks to Norwich to recover Bigod's body, but it was so well-guarded that their mission proved futile.

Although Prior Stephen made further efforts to retrieve Bigod's body, they proved negative, and Lady Alice had to submit to the will of Bishop de Losinga and agree that her husband should be officially buried in Norwich Cathedral.

THE BISHOPRIC OF ELY

In the early 12th century the Diocese of Lincoln was the largest in England, covering an area from the River Humber in the north to the Thames in the south, and from Ely in the east to Banbury in the west.

It was the ambition of Abbot Richard of Ely to create a bishopric from the huge diocese with himself as bishop of his newly-erected church at Ely raised to the status of a cathedral.

Abbot Richard was in high favour with the King and was one of his principal councillors. He proposed his plan of creating a new bishopric to the King, who agreed to the idea. The King sent messages to Rome to obtain the Pope's approval, but before the Pope came to a decision Richard fell sick and died on 16th June 1107. He was buried the following day in his new church.

When he heard of Abbot Richard's death, the Pope halted all proceedings for the formation of a new diocese, and the King installed Hervey le Breton as administrator of the affairs of Ely Abbey until a new abbot could be appointed.

Hervey had been a favourite chaplain of King William Rufus, and was appointed Bishop of Bangor in North Wales in 1092. Not known for his holiness, Hervey was chiefly appointed to subdue the Welsh to Norman rule rather than his interest in their spiritual well-being.

Being unfamiliar with their character, and ignorant of their language, he tried to subdue the Welsh by force of arms. But the Welsh retaliated by armed insurrection, killing Hervey's relatives. They also threatened to kill him if he fell into their hands. Hervey beat a hasty retreat to the King's court and anxiously petitioned the monarch to relieve him of his mission in wild Wales and appoint him to a less hazardous position.

As administrator of Ely Abbey he rigorously pursued the creation of a bishopric at Ely. His persistence was eventually rewarded when the Bishop of Lincoln gave consent to the division of his huge diocese.

The Pope sent letters in favour of the division, and in October 1109, King Henry granted a charter constituting the Bishopric of Ely and nominating Hervey le Breton as Bishop, and the great Abbey was downgraded to a Priory.

The King also ordered that all the monastery's estates should be equally divided between the bishop and monks. But when Bishop Hervey drew up the charter dividing the estates he ensured that the monks were granted the poorest lands, whilst he received the most valuable parts of the estate.

Hervey's purse consequently swelled by £1,040 a year, while the 70 monks received an annual income of only £300 between them. Although they complained bitterly about the injustice, they were forced to take what had been given them.

THE GREAT FIRE OF PETERBOROUGH

In 1114 the Archbishop of Canterbury appointed John de Seez of Normandy as Abbot of Peterborough, but the King ordered John to travel to Rome to collect the pallium – a woollen 'Y' shaped vestment – conferred on the

Archbishop by Pope Pascal, before he could take up residence in the Abbot's house.

When the monks of the abbey heard that their new Abbot would not be with them for a long time, the chronicler of the abbey recorded that they 'wept and shed many tears'. They probably regretted shedding tears when John de Seez returned from his mission to Rome in 1116, for they soon discovered that he had a sharp temper and quickly flew into a rage over the slightest incident that displeased him.

One day in August 1116, a servant failed to get a fire started in the bakehouse. Seeing his hopeless attempts, the Abbot lost his temper and bellowed; "Come Devil, blew the fire!" Almost at once the fire burst into life with a vengeance.

The flames shot up to the roof and set it on fire, then rapidly spread through the monastery buildings until it reached the great church, where it raged uncontrollably for nine days.

Monks escaping from the blazing abbey.

On the ninth night a strong wind arose and scattered red-hot cinders on to the Abbot's house and many other houses. Soon the whole town was reduced to a smouldering ruin. 'It was the Devil's doing", lamented the chronicler.

The Devil's doing or not, John de Seez spent the rest of his abbacy rebuilding the monastery. Although he worked hard, he did not live to see the formidable task completed, dying of dropsy in 1125.

EARTHQUAKE

When the learned Joffrid of Orleans arrived at Crowland Abbey on 1109 to take up his appointment as Abbot, he found the church in a ruinous state, never having been repaired after a disastrous fire in 1091, although the abbey was rich in funds.

Much of the abbey's wealth had been donated by pilgrims who visited the tomb of the Saxon Earl Waltheof, who they honoured as a saint. Joffrid decided that the abbey could well-afford to build a new church and set to work organising the re-building.

In 1114, at a ceremony, attended by 5,000 people, thirty-eight foundation stones were laid by invited dignitaries for the new church. After the ceremony, all 5,000 of those attending sat down to a sumptuous feast.

No doubt it was this feast that prompted a later writer to include the line, 'Crowland, the courteous of their meat and drink' in a ballad about Fen abbeys.

After the festivities the work continued in earnest under the direction of Odo the Prior. For four years the building work progressed steadily, until disaster struck in 1118. Suddenly the ground trembled, causing the unroofed north wall of the church to collapse, and the south wall to crack in so many places that it had to be shored up with beams.

Although shaken by the unusual occurrence, Joffrid and Odo were not deterred from their aim, and began the task of repairing and rebuilding the badly damaged structure of the new church again.

DEATH OF BISHOP DE LOSINGA

Herbert de Losinga, the first bishop of Norwich, had held the position for twenty-eight years when he died in his palace at Norwich at the age of 65 on 22nd July 1119. Revered for his good deeds he was interred before the High Altar in the cathedral that he had founded.

During his life, he had been prominent in the ecclesiastical world, being a learned student of theology and a scholar of the classics. He was also renowned for his eloquent and long sermons, and even wrote a treatise entitled, 'On the End of the World'.

But Herbert made many enemies due to his domineering character and inflexibility, although he served King Henry loyally, and held Queen Matilda in high esteem.

Queen Matilda, the former Princess Edith of Scotland, was much loved by the people, who affectionately dubbed her 'Good Queen Mold' – Mold being a nickname for Matilda.

She did much charitable work, and gained respect by washing the feet of lepers and kissing their hands. When she died suddenly at the age of 41 on May Day 1118, Herbert was one of the chief mourners in her funeral train.

He was no doubt inspired by Queen Matilda's example to establish the leper Chapel and Hospital of St. Mary Magdalen outside the city walls of

Norwich, and endowed the hospital with lands and revenue before his death in 1119.

WAR IN NORMANDY

Like his late father, King Henry was naturally cruel, and, determined to restore peace and order to his realm. He introduced a number of severe and repressive reforms to check and punish lawlessness.

His reforms were so successful that he became known as the 'Lion of Justice', and it was said that 'no man dare do ill to another in his time'.

He was also ambitious to unite Normandy and England under one monarch, and launched an attack on Normandy in 1106 to gain control.

Duke Robert's weak and ineffectual rule, combined with poor defences, eventually led to his defeat at the Battle of Tinchebrai. He was ignominiously sent to England in chains and imprisoned in Cardiff Castle for the rest of his life.

Henry assumed the title of Duke of Normandy, but in 1116, King Louis the Fat of France took up the cause of William Clito, the son of Duke Robert, who claimed his right to the Duchy of Normandy.

Once again King Henry, concerned about the threat to his acquired continental domains, embarked for Normandy prepared for battle. He was accompanied by several loyal barons from East Anglia, including William Bigod, Constable of Norwich Castle, Eudo de Rye, Constable of Colchester Castle, his wife, Lady Rohais and her brothers Richard FitzGilbert, Lord of Clare, and Roger de Clare, also William de Warenne of Acre, Earl of Surrey.

The King of France, and his Flemish allies, swept through Normandy with fire and sword. They were supported by several Norman nobles who were in favour of William Clito's claim to the Duchy, and joined forces with the invading French.

King Henry, finding himself surrounded by enemies, could not effectively retaliate, and resorted to diplomacy and bribery to gain support. But the response was gradual and hostilities continued for three years before the fortunes of war began to swing in his favour.

On 20th November 1119, the two armies met on the plain of Bremule. King Henry, having been persuaded to take part in the battle by William de Warenne, donned his armour and joined his cavalry.

Under the personal command of the two Kings the opposing cavalry fought fiercely hand-to-hand at close quarters. As the battle raged King Henry was attacked and struck on the head by the sword of a French knight named Count Crispin. Although the King's armour was thought to be impenetrable, the force of the blow drove part of the chain-mail into his head, creating a wound which bled profusely.

Forgetting his wound the infuriated Henry knocked Crispin of his horse with a single blow. Roger de Clare immediately rushed to the King's assistance and secured the French knight, who, along with many others, was taken prisoner. The French, realising that they were severely beaten, fled the battle field at full gallop, King Louis the Fat at the fore.

King Henry, recovering from his wound, made peace with the rebel Normans by offering them generous terms. King Louis was content to accept that Prince William, King Henry's son, was the rightful heir to the Duchy of Normandy.

THE HEARTBREAK OF LADY ROHAIS

As the court was preparing to return to England in 1120 after peace was established, Eudo de Rye, the Constable of Colchester Castle and one of the King's stewards, was taken ill and conveyed to Preaux Castle, where he died.

Eudo decreed in his will that he wished to be buried in the Abbey of St. John in Colchester, which he had founded. He also bequeathed his manor of Brightlingsea, 100 pounds in coin, his valuable gold ring, inset with a topaz, and his horse and mute, to the abbey. His body was conveyed to England, but his heartbroken widow, Lady Rohais, was forbidden, by her scheming brothers, Richard FitzGilbert and Roger de Clare, to leave Normandy and accompany her husband's body to its resting place in Colchester.

The brothers had plans for her future, mainly to raise their widowed sister to the position of Queen of England by marrying her to King Henry. But however much they tried to bring them together at every opportunity, King Henry was not interested in re-marrying.

Although he found Lady Rohais charming and admired her, his interest went no further, and Lady Rohais flatly refused to be used as a political pawn and shut herself away.

In isolation, she pined and grieved the loss of her departed husband until she became quite ill. It is said that she eventually died of a broken heart.

Her callous brothers ignored her dying wish that she should be laid to rest beside her husband in the church of St. John's Abbey, Colchester, and had her buried in Normandy.

THE WHITE SHIP DISASTER

After an absence of just over four years, King Henry sailed for England from the port of Barfluer on the morning of 18th November 1120. His son, Prince William, and his young courtiers, refused to travel with him, and made the most of their last day in Normandy by feasting and drinking in a local tavern, having chartered a vessel called The White Ship which was prepared ready to sail later the same day.

Having time to spare, the captain and crew of The White Ship were invited to join in the revelry by the young Prince, who supplied barrels of wine for their consumption.

The White Ship was reported to be the finest English vessel afloat at the time, but when it eventually set sail from Barfluer it was manned by a Captain and crew who were as drunk as their noble passengers.

But set sail it did, disastrously! A little way out of Barfluer, the swift currents drove the ship on to the rocks of the Cotentin Peninsula, tearing a huge hole in the hull. The vessel keeled over and sank.

With no help at hand, only one person, a butcher from Rouen, survived to tell the tale of how 300 others perished. Among the blue bloods lost were Prince William, Richard, Earl of Chester and his wife, and William Bigod, Constable of Norwich Castle.

King Henry was devastated by the news of the tragic death of his only son and heir. Hopes of continuing the Norman dynasty seemed to have come to an end with the sinking of The White Ship.

It is said that the King never smiled again, and one chronicler recorded that 'no ship ever brought such misery to England'.

His words would echo true in years to come.

THE KING AT NORWICH

Although King Henry had 22 children, 20 of them were bastards, born to his numerous mistresses, so that the loss of his only legitimate son, Prince William, was not only a personal tragedy, but posed a threat to the continuation of the Norman line of succession.

In 1121 he made the barons swear an oath of fealty to his legitimate daughter, the Empress Maud, wife of the Holy Roman Emperor Henry V, that they would support her succession to the throne.

The barons, however, insisted that King Henry marry again and try to produce a legitimate male heir. After recovering from his melancholia following the death of Prince William, Henry decided to marry Adelicia, the beautiful 18 year old daughter of the Count of Louvain.

Although Adelicia was not a Norman, she spoke French fluently and was accepted as a suitable bride for the King by the barons. The wedding took place at Windsor Castle on 29th January 1121.

In 1122 the King decided to spend the Christmas period at Norwich Castle. He issued instructions to Hugh Bigod. the Constable, to prepare for his stay. Hugh, at the age of twenty-eight, had unexpectedly succeeded to the office and all the family estates following his elder brother's death in The White Ship disaster.

Preparing for a royal visit was an enormous task, for the King did not travel lightly. Chamberlains, stewards, butlers, marshals, personal retainers, cooks, servants, clergy, musicians, jesters, guards, knights and men-at-arms, accompanied him in a train of wagons.

To accommodate and feed the large retinue, Bigod resorted to plundering the surrounding district for whatever provisions he could lay his hands on.

It was widely known that the King ate and drank moderately, but slept soundly and snored loudly, except when nightmares of his assassination disturbed him, when he would leap out of bed, grab the sword, which he always kept by his bedside, and furiously slash the enemies he had dreamed of.

The prospect of entertaining the King and his court for any lengthy period was looked upon with dread by the host, for apart from the major disruption, it could leave him bankrupt. But whatever problems were envisaged, the combined efforts of Hugh Bigod and the newly installed Bishop of Norwich, Eborard de Montgomery, succeeded in making the King's stay enjoyable.

King Henry was so impressed by the reception he received, and his enjoyable visit, that he granted the citizens of Norwich a charter, giving them the same liberties as those given to the citizens of London.

KING HENRY'S PILGRIMAGE

In 1121, Anselm, Abbot of the Monastery of St. Saba in Rome, was offered the vacant abbacy of Bury St. Edmunds. He accepted the position, and resigned his Roman abbacy before coming to England to take up his new office. A nephew of the late Archbishop Anselm of Canterbury, he was a highly educated and cultural man, and under his enlightened rule, the abbey soon became a centre of knowledge and learning.

The abbey gained further fame for its illuminated manuscripts, considered to be of unrivalled quality. The manuscripts were created in the abbey's scriptorium on vellum, a parchment made from the skins of calves, lambs or kids, and included volumes of Gospels, Psalters, and Sermons. The abbey's Library became renowned throughout England, its oldest and most prized possession being a copy of 'The life of St. Edmund'.

But the abbey's greatest claim to fame was the Shrine of St. Edmund, England's Patron Saint. There was always a regular flow of pilgrims intent on paying homage to the Saint, many of them sick or dying hoping for a miracle cure. Such was the reverence paid to Saint Edmund that King Henry visited his shrine in 1132.

The King, returning by ship from one of his numerous visits to Normandy was midway across the Channel when a storm suddenly blew up and the little ship was tossed so violently by huge waves that it was in danger of capsizing.

King Henry fell to his knees and vowed that if St. Edmund saved the ship he would make a pilgrimage to his shrine. The ship survived the storm, and Henry kept his vow.

Abbot Anselm must have been a good host, because the King was so impressed by the welcome he received and by the new abbey church, that two years later he issued a charter giving permission for the abbey to hold a fair, three days before and three days after the Festival of St. James.

THE LOATHSOME HUNTERS

In 1127 Pope Honorius II sent his legate to England to collect the annual Peter's Pence. This was a tax imposed by successive Popes to cover the administration costs of the Holy See of Rome. It was levied on all households where the yearly income exceeded thirty pence.

The Pope's legate on this occasion was Henry, Abbot of the Monastery of St. John Angeli in France. He was an ambitious fortune-hunter, who had entered into several adventurous schemes to obtain high office, but, although he had held several ecclesiastical positions, 'through his great trick', during his chequered career in France, he failed to hold them for any length of time due to his inadequacy and 'great stupidity'.

A cousin of the King of England, he was determined to use his position as collector of Peter's Pence in England, by visiting his royal relation when he was collecting the tax in London.

The King willingly received him and was impressed by Henry's sad story that he was an 'old and broken man' who could no longer endure the wars, hostilities and troubles that ensued in France. Henry told the King that he would love to spend the rest of his days in the peaceful Kingdom of England, and begged the King to give him the vacant abbacy of Peterborough.

King Henry was moved by the crafty Abbot's story, and granted the vacant abbacy of Peterborough to him on condition that he resigned the abbacy of St. John Angeli.

Abbot Henry readily agreed to the King's terms, but had no intention of keeping to his word once he had been installed as Abbot of Peterborough. His intention all along had been to have control of an abbey in England, as well as retaining control of the Abbey of St. John Angeli in France.

Having deceived the King, Henry de Angeli took up his appointment at Peterborough and set about collecting the Pope's tax. He received due homage from the knights and tenants of the abbey, but lost no time in stripping the clergy, laymen, and the abbey of whatever valuables he could, then sent the booty to his monastery in France.

Abbot Henry had arrived in Peterborough during the period of Lent, and, according to one chronicler, 'there occurred a terrible portent' at the time.

Many people claimed to have seen huntsmen in the deer park at

The building of the great abbey church at Peterborough, begun in 1125, came to a standstill under the rule of Abbot Henry de Angeli.

Peterborough, and in the woods between Peterborough and Stamford. They reported hearing the huntsmen's horns, and the howling of their hounds.

The hunters were 'black and huge and loathsome, and their hounds all black and wide eyed and loathsome, and they rode on black horses and on black billy-goats'. Curiously the sightings ended at Easter, and the mysterious huntsmen were never seen again.

In 1130, Peter, Abbot of Cluny, visited Peterborough and was greeted with honour by Abbot Henry. After formalities had ended, the two abbots spent time together thinking up a scheme whereby the two monasteries could be united under the Clunaic order and be subjective to the Abbot of Cluny.

When King Henry heard of this plan, he was furious at having been deceived by Henry de Angeli , and would not accept his excuses that the monks were to blame for the plan. He deposed Abbot Henry de Angeli from office and banished him from England.

CHAPTER FOUR

The Anarchy, 1133-1154

A DISH OF LAMPREYS

The traditional harvest festival in earlier church days was always celebrated on the 1st August, known as Lanmas Day, or Loaf Day, when freshly baked bread from the first ripened corn was consecrated at mass.

It was on this day in 1133 that King Henry set sail for Normandy to see his first grandchild, born to his daughter, the Empress Maud.

Maud had married Geoffrey the Handsome, Count of Anjou, in 1129, and their first child, a son, whom they named Henry, was born on 5th March 1133.

But, according to an old chronicle, nine days after King Henry left England, 'the sun became as if it were a three-night old moon'. What was a rare eclipse of the sun so terrified the people that they were convinced it was a sign of ill-fortune.

Undeterred by superstition, the King spent a few quiet days at his favourite hunting lodge near Rouen in pursuit of deer before the arrival of his daughter, her husband and their child.

His euphoria at seeing his grandson for the first time was short-lived when a bitter quarrel broke out between him and his hot-tempered daughter regarding the castles which formed part of her dowry.

Count Geoffrey demanded that they be handed over to him, but King Henry refused, adamant that he would control the castles as long as he lived. The furious Maud returned to Anjou with her husband and child, leaving her father heartbroken by the bitter disagreement.

The family problems weighed heavily upon the 67-year-old monarch's mind, and as a result, his health began to fail. After a meal on the 25th March 1135, in which he ate a large dish of lampreys, his favourite seafood, he complained of suffering from acute indigestion. But the severe stomach pains which followed were most likely caused by food poisoning.

His condition quickly deteriorated. A fever set in and, some days later, fearing his end was near, he confessed his sins to a priest. Many nobles were assembled at his bedside, and after mumbling a few incomprehensible words to them, he drew his last breath and died.

BIGOD THE KINGMAKER

Hugh Bigod had been standing nearest to the King when he died and said he had understood his last words, although they had seemed meaningless to the other nobles present. Bigod lost no time in hastening across the Channel to Canterbury after the King's death, where he swore on oath to the Archbishop that the King had disinherited his daughter, and had named his nephew, Stephen of Blois, as his successor.

Knowing that he was supported by Hugh Bigod, Stephen acted quickly to ensure he secured the throne. By the time he arrived in London, the citizens acclaimed him as their King, having been told by Bigod of the King's change of heart.

Stephen of Blois gained the throne of England by the testimony of Hugh Bigod. – PLAYERS CIGARETTE CARD.

The Empress Maud gained support from some East Anglian barons.

Stephen then journeyed to Winchester, where his brother, Henry of Blois, was Bishop, and gained the support of leading churchmen, particularly that of Roger, Bishop of Salisbury, who as Chief Justiciar, was the most powerful man in the land and virtually controlled the government of the realm.

The Archbishop of Canterbury, however, still wavered as he had been one of the first to have taken the oath of fealty to the Empress Maud.

Stephen was concerned, because only the Archbishop could anoint him King, but he was eventually won over after being convinced that the oath to Maud had been made under duress.

Stephen gained further favour with the Archbishop by promising more liberties for the Church, and was crowned King of England in Westminster Abbey on 22nd December 1135.

BIGOD THE BOLD

In 1136 King Stephen fell ill and rumour quickly spread that he had died. Hugh Bigod, on hearing the rumour, feared what consequences might ensue, particularly after he had perjured himself over Empress Maud's disinheritance, so he fled to Norwich and fortified the castle.

He felt relatively safe behind the newly-erected stone walls of the castle, and remained there waiting for political events to develop.

But the rumour of the King's death was untrue and he soon recovered from his illness. When he heard of Bigod's flight to Norwich, the King believed Bigod had changed his allegiance in favour of the Empress Maud, and dismissed him from the office of Constable and ordered him to vacate Norwich Castle.

Bigod, aggrieved at losing his rank of Royal Constable, and all the benefits that came with the position, refused to surrender the castle to anyone other than the King himself.

Stephen therefore journeyed to Norwich, and gathered an army on the way just in case Bigod caused trouble. When he arrived at Norwich, he must have been impressed by the sight of the new stone castle.

Towering over the city, it had been transformed into a formidable fortress, its white-stone keep on a massive motte. It could well have withstood a lengthy siege, but Hugh Bigod gave up the castle peacefully, thus avoiding inevitable bloodshed.

Hugh Bigod transformed the castle at Norwich into a formidable fortress. – LATE
NINETEENTH – EARLY TWENTIETH CENTURY POSTCARD.

Unlike his Norman predecessors, Stephen was not a cruel or vindictive
man, and readily forgave Bigod for his misdemeanour. The two appear to
have settled their differences with a compromise.

Stephen allowed Bigod to retire to his castle at Bungay and to retain one
third of the profits of the county, the other two thirds going to William of
Blois, as custodian of the castle.

William of Blois is referred to by historians of the time as the 'natural' son
of King Stephen, although there is no evidence to suggest that Stephen had a
bastard child called William before or after he married.

It is more likely that William of Blois was the second son of Stephen and
Matilda, his Queen. But William was a minor at the time he was made
Constable of Norwich Castle, so that may account for the responsibility of its
care being given to John de Chesney, the newly-appointed Sheriff of Norfolk,
who was a staunch supporter of King Stephen.

THE WARRIOR MONKS
Stephen had married Matilda, the daughter and heiress of Count Eustace of
Boulogne, in 1125. The Count, although resident on the continent, was a
substantial landowner in East Anglia, owning seventy manors in Essex as
well as lands in Cambridgeshire, Norfolk and Suffolk, all of which Matilda
inherited when her father died shortly after her marriage.

71

A Warrior Knight of the Order of the Knights Templar.

Matilda's wealth was impressive, as was her lineage. Saxon blood flowed in her veins as a descendent of King Ethelred the Unready of England and King Malcolm Canmore of Scotland.

The Boulogne family had played a major role in leading and financing the First Crusade to the Holy Land in 1095, and Matilda's uncles, Godfrey and Baldwin, were successively appointed Kings of the Crusader Kingdom of Jerusalem.

In 1118 a group of nine French knights formed a fraternity called The Poor Knights of Christ and The Temple of Solomon, their aim being to escort and protect pilgrims to the Holy City when they arrived at the coast. They were given quarters on the site of the temple and became known simply as The Knights Templar.

A French monk, named Bernard of Clairvaux, was elected to compile rules for the Templars. These included an allowance of three horses and one servant for each soldier-monk, the vow of poverty, obedience and chastity, and a pledge to fight to the death in order to protect the Holy Places and to give no mercy to the infidels.

In 1136, the Order of The Knights Templar was growing in popularity and the number of knights joining the Order had increased, causing financial crisis, and the need for them to seek a regular source of income.

Several of the original nine knights who formed the Order had ties with the Boulogne region of France, having been vassals of Matilda's father.

Concerned for the well-being of the Order, Queen Matilda eased their crisis by endowing the Knights with the rich agricultural manor of Cressing in Essex. Other nobles followed her lead, including King Stephen, who gave them the Essex town of Witham and the right to hold a weekly market there.

Within a few years the Knights Templar owned about fifty manors scattered across the counties of England, and many more in France, which collectively provided them with a considerable income.

ABBOT ANSELM'S AMBITIONS

A journey to the Holy Sepulchre in Jerusalem came first on every pilgrim's list of Holy places to visit in the Middle Ages. Second was St. Peter's Church in Rome.

The third, but by no means less popular place. was the burial place of St. James the Great, one of the twelve disciples of Christ, at Santiago de Compostela in northern Spain. Over a million pilgrims a year travelled across the Pyrenees to his shrine at the height of its popularity.

NORMAN TOWER AND CATHEDRAL CHURCH, BURY ST. EDMUNDS. K.195.

Abbot Anselm of Bury St. Edmunds felt compelled to visit this sacred site before he died, but after careful consideration the ageing Abbot had second thoughts about attempting such a long and hazardous journey. As a compromise he decided to honour the apostle by building a church in the abbey grounds and dedicating it to him.

The building of the church of St. James began in 1135, and Anselm intended that it should also serve the town of Bury as a parish church. A separate bell-tower gateway was also erected close to the church. This served the dual function of bell-tower to

The Bell-tower Gateway at Bury St. Edmunds, built for Abbot Anselm. – EARLY TWENTIETH CENTURY POSTCARD.

the church of St James and gateway to the Abbey Church and the shrine of St. Edmund.

In spite of his age and infirmities, Abbot Anselm also had designs on being Bishop of London, and lobbied hard to secure votes when Bishop Gilbert died in 1136 and King Stephen gave the Canons of the diocese freedom to elect the next bishop.

But Anselm was supported by only half of the Canons at the election. Not to be thwarted in his ambition to secure the bishopric of London, he gathered a force of knights and seized Waytemore Castle near Stortford, Hertfordshire, the fortified residence of the Bishop of London, in a brash bid to intimidate the electors.

Anselm's high-handed action in occupying the castle proved to be a mistake, for his opponents were aggravated and appealed to the Pope for help.

When the matter eventually came to the attention of Pope Innocent the Second in 1138, he wanted more information and asked Thurstan, Archbishop of Canterbury, for his opinion.

Thurstan was obviously opposed to the promotion of Anselm, for he replied that 'it would be more fitting to remove him from his abbacy than promote him as Bishop of London'. The Pope took heed of Thurstan's reply and annulled the election, temporarily appointing the Bishop of Winchester to administer the diocese until a new bishop was elected.

Anselm smarting from his failed bid for promotion, withdrew to Bury where he remained Abbot until his death in 1146, claiming to be the rightful Bishop of London to the last.

William of the Strong Arm featured a tongueless lion for his coat of arms.

WILLIAM OF THE STRONG HAND

William de Albini the Younger, like his maternal grandfather, Roger Bigod, grew up to be a great warrior and was much admired by the ladies as one of the most glamorous knights of his day. But unlike his grandfather Bigod, he was chivalrous and courteous in his conduct. Late in 1137 William travelled to Bourges in France to take part in a tournament that was held as one of the public events to celebrate the coronation of King Louis the Young and his wife, Queen Eleanor.

The castle at Rising, built by William of the Strong Arm for his wife, the dowager Queen Adelicia. – EARLY TWENTIETH CENTURY POSTCARD BY JEWSON'S, KING'S LYNN.

Tournaments had become a popular form of entertainment by then. The jousting contests were also considered excellent training for warrior-knights, although several knights lost their lives because real weapons were used in the contests in order to make them as realistic and exciting as possible.

The Church strongly objected to tournaments on moral grounds, but regardless of Pope Innocent banning them as early as 1130, they continued to flourish.

William proved to be a great warrior, beating all his opponents in the contests to take the prize. All who witnessed the contests were impressed with his strength, skill and courage, none more so than Adelaide of Savoy, the Dowager-Queen of France, who instantly lost her heart to him.

Adelaide blatantly conveyed a message to William that she wished to marry him, but William turned her offer down, saying that he had 'pledged his troth' to Adelicia of Louvain, Dowager-Queen of England.

The chroniclers of the time record that Adelaide was furious at being rejected and was jealous of anyone else gaining William's hand in marriage, and plotted revenge on him for turning her down.

She invited William to visit her for a talk, and lured him into her garden where she had previously set free a hungry lion. Seeing a stranger in the garden, the lion attacked William, much to Adelaide's delight. But William, according to chronicles, seized the lion by the throat, thrust his hand into its mouth and ripped out its tongue. The lion, roaring in agony, retreated to nurse his wound, and Adelaide withdrew to her palace to nurse her wounded pride.

After his incredible victory over the lion, William was given the surname 'of The Strong Hand', and returned to England in 1138 to marry the beautiful Adelicia, who had withdrawn from public life to her castle at Arundel on the Sussex coast following the death of her first husband, King Henry I.

Here, far from the intrigues of court life, William came to reside with his chosen bride. But not long after his marriage to Adelicia, William's father died and he inherited large estates in Norfolk, including his father's castle at Old Buckenham.

The castle was considered unsuitable as a residence for a former queen, so William decided to erect a more luxurious residence in his manor of Rising, near Lynn, where they could stay when visiting their estates in East Anglia.

INTRIGUE AT ELY

Two years elapsed after the death of Hervey, the first Bishop of Ely, before King Henry decided to appoint a successor. He eventually chose his trusty treasurer, Nigel le Poer, who was consecrated on 1st October 1133.

Nigel's appointment to the position was undoubtedly due to the influence of his powerful uncle Roger, Bishop of Salisbury, who, as Chief Justiciar, practically ran the administration of the country.

Because of his high office of state, Nigel was obliged to reside in London, so he appointed Ranulph, a secular clergyman, to manage the affairs of the diocese.

After King Henry's death, Ranulph appears to have become the central figure in a mysterious plot to fortify the Isle of Ely in support of an Angevin invasion, which intended to replace King Stephen as monarch with Empress Maud.

When rumour spread that Stephen had died in 1136, the plot prematurely came into the open. But the rumour proved false, and when he heard that King Stephen was very much alive, Ranulph fearing for his life, seized what treasure he could and took flight.

Whether Bishop Nigel was involved in the plot is uncertain, although King Stephen harboured doubts about his loyalty.

THE BISHOP OF ELY'S ESCAPE

Bishop Roger of Salisbury continued to serve as Chief Justiciar under King Stephen, and, together with his nephews, Nigel and Alexander, respectively Bishops of Ely and Lincoln, and his illegitimate son, Roger le Poer, who was Chancellor of England, virtually controlled the government of the kingdom.

They also controlled several well-fortified castles, and retained a large army of knights who would respond to their commands.

Many barons were fearful of such power concentrated in one family, and informed the King of their suspicions that Bishop Roger was secretly planning to support Empress Maud's claim to the throne, and advised Stephen to break the power of the bishops.

The King took notice of them, and called a Council of Barons at Oxford on 24th June 1139. The three bishops and Chancellor Roger were also summoned to attend.

Their arrival at Oxford was accompanied by an enormous retinue of servants and retainers, plus a large force of men-at-arms and mounted knights. This show of military strength caused the King to suspect treason, and, according to one chronicler, to order his men-at-arms to be ready for battle.

The atmosphere was tense throughout the meeting, and eventually led to a skirmish between the three bishops' forces and those of the Earl of Richmond, during which one soldier was killed and several more wounded.

This gave the King the excuse he needed to order the arrest of the three bishops and Chancellor Roger, on the charge of Breaking the King's Peace. Bishops Roger and Alexander, and the Chancellor, were subsequently arrested in their lodgings.

Nigel, having lodgings outside the town, escaped to the Bishop of Salisbury's castle at Devizes when he heard the news of the arrests, because, it is said, he had 'a guilty conscience'.

Devizes Castle was held by Matilda of Ramsbury, mistress of the Bishop of Salisbury. When Bishop Nigel arrived he found it well-prepared to withstand a long siege.

Nigel's action was seen by King Stephen as confirmation of the treasonable intentions of the bishops, and he set off for Devizes in pursuit of Nigel, taking two of his prisoners, namely Bishop Roger and Chancellor Roger, with him.

Finding Devizes Castle strongly defended upon arrival, and having no time for a long siege, the King threatened to hang the Chancellor from a high gallows just outside the gates of the castle if the occupants refused to surrender.

Bishop Nigel, with complete disregard for the consequences of his rebellious action, appears to have been quite prepared to see his cousin hang, but Matilda of Ramsbury, Chancellor Roger's mother, understandably was not, telling the obstinate Bishop Nigel, "I gave him birth, and it cannot be right for me to cause his destruction."

After three days of holding out, she agreed to surrender the castle if the

King would free her son and Bishop Roger. King Stephen agreed to Matilda's terms.

He also apparently forgave Bishop Nigel and allowed him to return to Ely, although he did confiscate his and the other bishops' castles and their hoarded wealth, which collectively amounted to the huge sum of 40,000 marks.

EARL WILLIAM'S GUEST

On 30th September 1139, Empress Maud landed on the Sussex coast with her half-brother, Robert, Earl of Gloucester, and a force of 140 knights.

Robert, who had visited Maud in Anjou, no doubt to discuss plans that would lead to her replacing King Stephen on the throne of England, marched across England with 40 knights via 'hidden ways' to Bristol, where he was joined by several rebellious barons of the West Country.

Meanwhile, Maud was received at Arundel Castle by her step-mother, the Dowager-Queen Adelicia and her husband, William of the Strong Hand, Earl of Sussex.

When King Stephen heard the news that the Empress Maud had landed in England and was residing at Arundel Castle, he gathered a large armed force, marched to the castle, and demanded its surrender.

Although Arundel Castle was a strong fortification, it was occupied by only a small force of soldiers, who were ill-prepared for war.

When Adelicia saw King Stephen's large army outside her gates, she realised that harbouring Maud could be considered treasonable, and eager to stress that both she and her husband remained loyal, she pointed out to King Stephen that her step-daughter had only been received and accommodated as a family guest.

Whether he was gullible, or of an easily forgiving nature, King Stephen surprisingly allowed his rival, Empress Maud, and her knights, freedom to join her half-brother, Earl Robert, in Bristol, and withdrew his forces from Arundel Castle, a decision that he was later to regret.

'A MAN OF BLOOD'

When Bishop Nigel of Ely heard that the Empress Maud was gathering supporting forces in the West Country, he openly declared himself to be in favour of her cause, and began to fortify the Isle of Ely.

He strengthened Ely Castle, which he had regained by devious means, with 'stone and cement', and then with a band of hired knights, in true baronial style, began to plunder and pillage the surrounding area. In the words of one chronicler, Nigel became 'a man of blood'.

With rebellions breaking out in several places across the country, King

Stephen was faced with the dilemma of deciding which one to counter first. For some reason he decided to march on Ely and put down the comparatively minor rebellion of Bishop Nigel, instead of the more serious and threatening gathering of Empress Maud's forces in the West Country.

Upon arrival in the Cambridgeshire Fens with his large army, Stephen was faced with the same difficulties as his grandfather, William the Conqueror, had confronted years earlier when quelling the rebellion of Hereward the Saxon.

The marsh and swamps surrounding the island of Ely were virtually impenetrable. To transport his forces across them, Stephen had to build a temporary bridge made of boats positioned side by side, layered with hurdles on the top to form a crude crossing.

He then employed a monk, named Daniel from Ramsey Abbey, to guide his army across the island to Ely Castle, taking Bishop Nigel and his garrison by surprise. After a fierce struggle, during which many of the bishop's knights were either killed or taken prisoner, the castle was taken.

Bishop Nigel, having realised that he was defeated, fled from Ely in a boat, 'a poor and humbled man', and made his way to Gloucester to join the Empress Maud.

King Stephen was nevertheless elated with his capture of the island of Ely and the vast amount of treasure and booty that Bishop Nigel had stashed away, and rewarded the monk Daniel for his services with the promise of the Abbacy of Ramsey when it should fall vacant.

BIGOD BESIEGED

Hugh Bigod, angered by his eviction from Norwich Castle, also declared his support for Empress Maud when he learned of her landing, and immediately strengthened and garrisoned his castle at Bungay.

Once again King Stephen decided to march into East Anglia with a large army, and they arrived at Bungay on Whit Sunday 1140.

Bungay acquired its name from the Norman term 'le bon eye,' meaning 'a good island,' as the small town and its castle was practically surrounded by the meandering River Waveney.

Although the castle was situated in a good defensive position, it is doubtful whether an actual siege took place, for it seems likely that the King's threatening army was cause enough to persuade Bigod to capitulate and come to terms with the King.

Stephen, anxious to gain the loyalty and support of one of the most powerful barons of East Anglia, again forgave Bigod and allowed him to keep his castle. As a further incentive to secure his loyalty, he created him Earl of Norfolk.

THE BATTLE OF LINCOLN

Early in 1141 King Stephen gathered a small force, which included three contingents from East Anglia under the command of Hugh Bigod, Earl of Norfolk, William de Warenne, Earl of Surrey, and Gilbert de Clare, the newly created Earl of Hertford. The small force marched on Lincoln with the intention of laying siege to the castle, which was occupied by supporters of Empress Maud.

Stephen was unaware that while he was besieging Lincoln, his enemies in the West Country were assembling a vast army, which included 'a dreadful and unendurable mass of Welshmen' under the command of Robert, Earl of Gloucester,

They were swelled in numbers by another rebellious army, assembled by the Earl of Chester, who joined them on the march to Lincoln.

King Stephen was completely taken by surprise when the Earl of Gloucester's army crossed the River Witham near Lincoln on 1st February, and hastily made ready to attack him.

Although his small force was heavily outnumbered and ill-prepared, the King was determined to stand his ground and fight, and the opposing armies met in a decisive battle the following day. In the first encounter, the Royalist cavalry charged into the poorly-armed Welsh mercenaries, and, after a fierce fight, the Welsh fled the field of battle.

Gilbert de Clare, Earl of Hertford, a loyal supporter of King Stephen during the Anarchy.

Flushed with success, the Royalists had no time to re-group before Earl Robert's cavalry charged into them after the disorganised Welsh fled, causing the Royalists to panic and scatter in all directions.

Realising their position was hopeless against such overwhelming odds, Hugh Bigod, William de Warenne and Gilbert de Clare, made their escape from the conflict and left the King to his fate.

Although his small band of men were completely surrounded, the King 'fought like a lion,' slaying the enemy with his sword until it broke in his hands. A loyal citizen from

Lincoln promptly gave him a battle-axe, and he fought on, almost alone, until he fell to the ground, struck by a stone thrown by one of the rebel soldiers.

He was immediately seized by his enemies and dragged before the Earl of Gloucester, who gave instructions that he was to be kept alive and unharmed, and taken to Bristol Castle in chains and incarcerated there.

LADY OF THE ENGLISH

With the King chained up in Bristol Castle, the Empress Maud quickly secured the royal treasury at Winchester, and then began her triumphant procession to London. Crowds flocked to see her along the route, and she entered London in triumph as they cheered and welcomed her as their queen.

The Empress was greeted by Aubrey de Vere, Lord Great Chamberlain of England, who had been quick to change sides after the King's defeat, and Geoffrey de Manderville, Earl of Essex, who, as Constable of the Tower, handed her the keys of that mighty fortress. For his loyalty Geoffrey was appointed Sheriff of Essex and Hertfordshire.

Maud settled into the Palace of Westminster, taking the title 'Lady of the English,' but insisted on the styles and trappings of her former imperial life, and continued to use the title of Empress. Her close supporters and attendants soon discovered that she had a strong, overbearing personality, and was a proud and arrogant virago who gave orders in a deep masculine voice. One chronicler commented that 'swollen with insufferable pride, she listened to no-one's advice'.

One of her first acts was to impose a high tax on Londoners to help pay for the upkeep of her army. The outraged Londoners, pleading poverty, took their complaint direct to the Empress, but the deputation soon got a taste of her autocracy.

A chronicler described the scene thus: 'with a grim look, her forehead wrinkled into a frown, every trace of a woman's gentleness removed from her face, she blazed into intemperate fury'.

The same chronicler stated that 'the citizens went away gloomy to their homes'. But when they heard the news that Queen Matilda had raised an army in Kent and was marching on London, they armed themselves and rose in rebellion.

They attacked the followers and supporters of the Empress Maud, and many were slain defending the Royal Palace, including Aubrey de Vere, but by the time they broke into the apartments of the Empress, she had fled.

AUBREY THE GRIM

Deserted by many of her followers, Empress Maud fled to Oxford and there began to muster her wavering supporters by offering them generous bribes.

Aubrey de Vere, known as the Grim, a supporter of the Empress Maud.

Following the death of his father, Aubrey de Vere III, known as 'the Grim' because of the stern expression he always wore, remained loyal to the Empress. As a result she confirmed upon him all the titles and estates of his father, including that of Lord Great Chamberlain of England.

She also made him Lord of the town and castle of Colchester, an office which he was never to take up because Colchester was held by Hamo de St Claire, who remained loyal to imprisoned King Stephen and was by no means prepared to surrender the town and castle to Empress Maud.

With no hope of taking possession of the Colchester stronghold, Aubrey decided to build a new and more magnificent castle at Hedingham by replacing the old wooden structure, which had been erected by his grandfather, with one built from stone.

THE EARL OF ESSEX CHANGES SIDES

Queen Matilda's army's march on London was practically unopposed and she entered the city in triumph. Geoffrey de Manderville, Earl of Essex, quickly realised that it would be advantageous to support her, and had no conscience about abandoning Empress Maud. He willingly gave up the keys of the Tower of London to Queen Matilda, and swore allegiance to her.

Geoffrey de Manderville's grandfather, a Norman knight, also named Geoffrey, was awarded 49 manors in Essex by the Conqueror. Geoffrey inherited all these estates on the death of his father, including the strong castle at Saffron Walden, which became his chief residence in Essex.

A further 29 estates were inherited from his mother, the daughter of Eudo de Rye, and an advantageous marriage to Rohese de Vere, sister of Aubrey the Grim, brought him even more estates as part of Rohese's marriage settlement. The accumulated estates made him one of the wealthiest and largest landowners in Essex.

A bold and brave knight, Earl Geoffrey could have played an important part in the service of his country, but he was ambitious, greedy and utterly unscrupulous, declaring loyalty to whichever side could best further his own interests and give him more power during the troubled times.

With London securely in the hands of the Royalists, Queen Matilda, 'forgetting the weakness of her sex', rallied her supporters, and with the 'valour of a man' led her army of a thousand Londoners, all magnificently attired in coats of mail and helmets, with intent to capture the city of Winchester, which had remained loyal to Empress Maud.

The Queen left Earl Geoffrey in command of the Tower of London, and instructed him to secure the road from London to Winchester, and to keep it open for communications and supplies.

WILLIAM DE WARENNE'S GREAT PRIZE

Empress Maud, supported by her half-brother, Robert, Earl of Gloucester, decided to move her army south to relieve the besieged city and castle of Winchester. But she had underestimated the strength of Matilda's army and her determination.

A fierce and bloody battle ensued when the two armies met, but Matilda's superior forces eventually routed Empress Maud's army, and she fled from the battle, narrowly escaping capture by the victorious Royalists.

Earl Robert also managed to withdraw from the battle with the survivors of his elite force, with the aim of commanding the road to Gloucester and form a rear-guard to protect his retreating half-sister.

But eight miles north-west of Winchester, near a bridge across the River Test, he found he was surrounded on all sides by an army of Flemish mercenaries under the command of Earl William de Warenne.

He fought bravely against overwhelming odds, but his small force was soon crushed and he had no choice but to surrender himself to Earl William.

William de Warenne proudly delivered Robert to Queen Matilda, who ordered that he

Geoffrey de Manderville, the Robber Baron, from the effigy on his tomb in the Temple Church, London.

should be imprisoned in Rochester Castle in Kent, but that he should be treated kindly.

Matilda now held Maud's chief military commander and Maud held King Stephen, so the situation remained at stalemate for a while, until the two sides agreed to negotiations, which took place on 1st November 1141, when both sides agreed to an exchange of prisoners. King Stephen's release was greeted with enthusiasm by the people, and his popularity increased when he was re-crowned King at Canterbury on Christmas Day.

The civil war had taken an incredible toll on the country. Fields had been left unsown, which led to famine, and the absence of law and order gave reign to gangs of bandits roaming the land and spreading terror.

Although Stephen was extremely grateful to his wife, Matilda, for her prominent part in securing his freedom from imprisonment, he was now faced with the problems of stamping out rebellion and restoring order to his troubled kingdom.

A DIVIDED KINGDOM

King Stephen's popularity was strengthened by the support of many of the barons who had deserted the awesome Empress Maud. An old chronicler records that after Stephen's coronation at Canterbury 'the people received him with great rejoicing'.

The people may have been glad enough to make the most of a State occasion, but they had little else to rejoice over. The land had been ravaged by famine, pillaged by bandits and freebooters, split by divided loyalties, and was practically lawless.

Empress Maud still had ambitions of regaining the throne, and spent her time behind the strong walls of Oxford Castle scheming how she could do so, while her half-brother, Earl Robert, rallied the few supporters she had left.

King Stephen, facing numerous problems, also rallied his supporters, he was determined to restore law and order to his Kingdom and end the evil war that had torn it apart.

He forgave Geoffrey de Manderville for his transgressions, and ensured his allegiance by granting him custody of the Tower of London, as well as giving him lands in Essex worth £400. He also made him Sheriff and Justiciar of Essex, Hertfordshire, Middlesex and London, and confirmed his title of Earl of Essex. As a further inducement to secure his loyalty, he gave Geoffrey permission to build a castle wherever he pleased on his lands.

Many East Anglian nobles, including, William de Warenne. Earl of Surrey, Gilbert de Clare, Earl of Hertford and William of the Strong Hand, Earl of Sussex, had become King Stephen's most loyal supporters.

Nigel, the Bishop of Ely, aware of the hopelessness of Empress Maud's position, endeavoured to make peace with the King, even though the Isle of Ely was still fortified by a large force of the bishop's knights. Stephen decided to forgive Nigel for supporting the Empress, but only re-instated him as bishop after he had sent the Earl of Pembroke to Ely to disband the bishop's army.

Hugh Bigod, the rebellious Earl of Norfolk, who had changed sides more than once during the anarchy, was not so easily won over. Bigod decided to lie low and await further developments, strengthening his castles at Bungay and Framlingham, before committing himself to one side or the other.

RIVAL ABBOTS

Since 1133 the monastery of Ramsey had been ruled by Abbot Walter, described as 'a man of gentle and pious habits', who, nevertheless, had created discord between himself and his brethren by siphoning part of the monastery's wealth for the benefit of himself and his family.

In an attempt to placate his brethren, the pious embezzler, who preferred to spend his days in prayer and quiet contemplation, appointed a monk named Daniel to manage the affairs of the abbey. Daniel was the same monk who, only two years earlier, had guided King Stephen and his army onto the island of Ely.

The guileful Daniel had ambitions to oust his master from the abbatical chair, and by persuasion and trickery managed to induce Walter to resign by convincing him that he would be able to spend more of his time in prayer.

Consequently, Abbot Walter, followed by Brother Daniel, set off for Stamford where the King was staying. There Walter went through the formalities of resigning his position by surrendering his staff of office to the King.

The King, remembering the great service that Daniel had performed for him at Ely, had no hesitation appointing him the new Abbot of Ramsey.

The tenants of the abbey were saddened by the loss of their pious Abbot, and rebuked him for allowing Daniel to so easily persuade him to resign. Their feelings and distress caused him to regret his hasty decision.

The arms of the Abbot of Ramsey.

After deep contemplation, Walter realised that he had been tricked out of office, and decided to set off for Rome and appeal to the Pope to restore his position of Abbot.

TREASON

Included in the many lands awarded to Geoffrey de Manderville, Earl of Essex, by King Stephen, was the manor of Pleshey, an estate that had previously formed part of the lands Queen Matilda had inherited from her father, the Count of Boulogne.

Geoffrey had chosen Pleshey as the chief seat of his domains, and built a mighty castle there, which he thought would be befitting to his wealth, power and position. He had risen to become one of the most powerful nobles in the country.

According to one chronicler, he had so much power that 'everywhere in the Kingdom, he took the King's place' and was so feared that he 'received more obedience than the King'.

But Geoffrey was still not satisfied. Wealth and power went to his head, greed and ambition became the driving force in his life. He even began to harbour the notion that he could 'bestow the Kingdom' on the Empress Maud, to his own advantage, and began to play a dangerous game.

While he outwardly appeared to support the King, Geoffrey secretly met the Empress at Oxford and continued to furtively correspond with her. But the King disturbed by his growing power and influence began to mistrust him.

When he discovered proof of Geoffrey's treason, he was furious and summoned the Earl to a Council held in St Alban's Abbey.

The King openly accused Geoffrey of plotting with the Empress to overthrow him, and called upon him to answer the charge. Geoffrey answered by laughing contemptuously at the King, turned his back on him, left the meeting and rushed out of the abbey to make his getaway.

But the King's soldiers and mounted knights, under the command of Earl William de Warenne, were prepared for such an eventuality. When they saw Geoffrey flee from the abbey to join his entourage they rallied to prevent his escape.

After a brief tussle, during which William de Warenne was unhorsed and fell to the ground, Earl Geoffrey was secured. He was put under arrest and escorted back to London by William de Warenne, who was unhurt by his fall.

When the escorting party arrived back in London, King Stephen gave Earl Geoffrey the choice of either being hanged or surrendering the Tower and his castles at Walden and Pleshey to him.

Geoffrey, repelled at the idea of ending his life on the gallows, chose the latter option. The King then foolishly gave him his freedom, but Geoffrey 'rent with rage', stormed from the King's presence 'like a vicious and riderless horse, kicking and biting', and fled north to Cambridgeshire with his knights.

SACRILEGE

Geoffrey de Manderville and his group of knights, having reached the safety of the Fens, established a camp at Fordham, near Newmarket on the Cambridgeshire – Suffolk border.

With help from his brother-in-law, William de Say, and support from Hugh Bigod, Earl of Norfolk, he built up a large force, consisting mainly of outlaws, robbers, soldiers of fortune and mercenaries, and planned to capture and fortify the Isle of Ely.

Meanwhile, Bishop Nigel was on a visit to Rome. He had been accused of inciting civil war and of squandering the income of his bishopric on an army of knights. Bishop Nigel transported as much treasure as he could carry and presented it to Pope Lucius II, thus influencing him to absolve Nigel of the charge.

During Nigel's prolonged absence, Geoffrey gained the support of William, the ageing Prior of Ely and his monks, who guided his army of ruffians across the hidden causeway onto the island of Ely.

Geoffrey took the castle at Ely with ease, also the important fortification at Aldreth, which guarded the southern approaches to the Isle, and garrisoned them. His next plan of action was to seize the rich Abbey of Ramsey.

On a cold December morning in 1143, Geoffrey and his army successfully set off across the treacherous swamps in boats without any serious mishap. They took the sleeping monks by surprise when the army invaded the abbey.

The monks were dragged from their beds and turned out of the abbey still in their night attire. Abbot Daniel, who had acquired the position by cunning, was also rudely awakened from his slumbers and thrown out into the fens.

Geoffrey's merciless army of ruffians, then stripped the abbey of every valuable ornament and sacred vessel made of gold or silver- an orgy of pillage and destruction. The abbey was then converted into a fortress, the cloisters transformed into stables for the knights horses, and the church became a dormitory for the soldiers.

In the words of one chronicler, they 'converted the sanctuary of God into the habitation of the Devil'. It was said that the walls of the abbey church 'exuded real blood' at such wanton acts of sacrilege.

The church leaders of England were enraged when they heard of the desecration of Ramsey Abbey, and at the instigation of Henry de Blois, Bishop of Winchester, they had no hesitation in passing excommunication on Geoffrey de Manderville, thus denying him the rites of the Holy Church.

TERROR IN THE FENS

Excommunication from the rites of the Roman Church meant little or nothing to Geoffrey de Manderville. He vented his anger on those he considered responsible for seizing his lands and castles, and had no qualms about making others suffer in order to obtain his ends.

He consequently set out with his band of marauders from his refuge in Ramsey Abbey to plunder and pillage the surrounding villages. With Rainer, his ruthless commander of the foot soldiers, he went from village to village, plundering and ransacking the houses, dragging away many of the inhabitants and holding them prisoner, subjecting them to torture until they agreed to pay a ransom.

One chronicler described the terrible tortures inflicted upon them thus: "They hung them up by the feet and smoked them with foul smoke. They hung them by the thumbs, or by the head, and hung heavy mail-coats on their feet. They put knotted strings around their heads and twisted till it went to their brains."

Encountering no opposition, Geoffrey became more daring and ventured further south to ransack and pillage Chatteris and St. Ives. Rainier and his soldiers ransacked and desecrated the monasteries, 'and spared neither church nor churchyard, nor did they spare abbots or monks'.

The townsfolk of Cambridge, fearing that the Earl might attack their town next, gathered together treasures and locked them in the vaults of the town's churches for safety.

As expected, Geoffrey attacked Cambridge, but the heavy bolted doors of the churches were scant obstacles to his determined soldiers. They smashed them down with their battering rams, entered the churches, took all the treasures, then set the churches alight.

Flushed with success, they went on to pillage the town, seizing what valuables they could and terrorising the inhabitants. They then set the town ablaze and fled deserted Cambridge for their haven in the Fens.

DEATH OF THE ROBBER BARON

When King Stephen heard of the depredations of rebel Earl Geoffrey, he, with his army, marched into Cambridgeshire. Geoffrey, however, safely encamped in the Fens, was reluctant to engage in battle with the King's forces.

Knowing the King's army would not dare to attempt to cross the treacherous marshy territory of the Fens, he chose to use guerrilla tactics, suddenly attacking the King's forces, then retreating into the safety of his camp at Ramsey.

The frustrated King eventually decided that the only way to crush Geoffrey's rebellion was to contain him in the Fens by constructing a series of castles around the fen's edges and wait for him to break out of his encampment.

One of the first castles the monarch set about constructing was at Burwell, where several houses had to be demolished to make way for it. The King's intention was to disrupt Geoffrey's supply line, but when news of the construction reached Geoffrey, he mustered his forces and left Ramsey Abbey in September 1144 with the idea of attacking Burwell before the castle could be completed.

When they were halfway across the Fens, Geoffrey halted his soldiers in a wood to rest so that they would be refreshed to engage in battle when they reached Burwell. It is said that when Geoffrey laid down to rest in the shade of a tree, ' the grass wilted and died under his unhallowed form'.

Whether that was so is incidental, but, having rested, Geoffrey gathered his army and moved on to Burwell. After arriving, he removed his helmet and loosened his chain-mail coat to ease himself from the heat of the day, whilst surveying the castle to determine the best direction to attack.

It was a careless error! A watching bowman, positioned on the partially built wall of the castle, seized the opportunity to let fly an arrow, which struck Geoffrey in the head.

The wound was thought not to be serious at first, so his loyal followers decided to carry him to Thetford, where Hugh Bigod might afford him help and protection. But the wound proved more severe than they realised, and Geoffrey died soon after they reached Mildenhall.

He died, excommunicated by the church, on 14th September 1144, so could not be buried in consecrated ground, but a passing group of Knights Templar took pity on his lifeless body, covered it with one of their white cloaks, emblazoned with a red cross, and conveyed it to London. There they placed it in a leaden coffin and suspended it in the branches of a crab-apple tree in the Templar's Holborn orchard. It remained there for twenty years until the Pope granted the dead Earl absolution. The Knights Templar then buried Geoffrey's body in their churchyard at Holborn.

RAMSEY RESTORED

Walter, the former Abbot of Ramsey, who had been tricked into resigning his office by monk Daniel, had journeyed to Rome and, after appealing to the Pope, who was impressed by Walter's 'pious and dove-like nature', restored him to his position as Abbot.

But upon his return to England, he found Ramsey Abbey still held by the rebels, and was forced to wander homeless over the abbey's lands, seeking shelter wherever he could, until the rebels were defeated.

Fortunately for Walter, Ernulf de Manderville, the eldest son of Earl

Geoffrey, soon realised the hopelessness of holding on to the abbey after his father's death and surrendered to King Stephen, thus ending the rebellion. Walter and his brother monks were then able to return to the abbey. But the monks were shocked by the ruinous state of the monastery, and of the desolation of the surrounding countryside.

For miles around the monastery the villages lay burnt and deserted, and the few peasants who had survived were suffering from disease and famine, their cattle and sheep having been killed, their fields lay barren. Even the dead had not been given a Christian burial, many were left unburied, half-eaten by maggots and wild beasts.

Walter immediately set about restoring the abbey, and its impoverished lands, bringing relief to the district's disillusioned inhabitants. It took many years, but by the time of Abbot Walter's death in 1161, Ramsey Abbey had been restored to its former glory.

Meanwhile, King Stephen once more treated his enemies leniently. Instead of ordering the execution of imprisoned Ernulf de Manderville, he disinherited him from his lands and title of Earl of Essex, and banished him from the realm.

MURDER AT NORWICH

Early in 1144, during Passion Week, the body of a boy was found in Thorpe Wood, near Norwich. Marks on his hands and feet suggested that he had been ritualistically nailed to a cross and crucified in a bizarre reconstruction of the Crucifixion of Christ.

The murder would have undoubtedly remained unsolved had it not been for the boy's uncle Godwine, a priest, who preached a sermon at a Synod of the clergy of the diocese, held in Norwich Cathedral in April of that year.

In his sermon to the assembly, Godwine referred to the murder of his nephew and accused the Jews of Norwich of the crime, although he had no firm evidence.

He recounted that his wife had had a dream, in which she was attacked by the Jews, who severed one of her legs and carried it away.

This he interpreted as proof that the Jews had selected and kidnapped his nephew as a victim for the crucifixion ritual to demonstrate their contempt of the worship of Jesus Christ by Christians.

Some members of the assembled congregation were impressed by Godwine's sermon, but Eborard de Montgomery, the Bishop of Norwich, was not convinced that the Jews were responsible for the boy's death. Nevertheless, he summoned the Jewish leaders to appear before the assembled clergy to answer the charges made against them.

At the time, all Jews in England were under the direct protection of the

The body of William of Norwich became a sacred relic and was reburied in the cathedral. – EARLY TWENTIETH CENTURY POSTCARD.

King, so when John de Chesney, the Sheriff of Norfolk, heard of the bishop's summons, he pointed out to him that he had no jurisdiction over the Jews.

Consequently, the Jewish leaders refused to appear before the Synod. Nevertheless, rumours of Godwine's accusation had spread throughout Norwich. It was supported by Elviva, the murdered boy's mother, who ran hysterical through the streets of Norwich calling out that the Jews had murdered her son.

Her behaviour incited a public outcry against the Jews, and mobs began to gather in the streets bent on seeking revenge on 'the enemies of Christ'.

Spurred on by support, Godwine repeated his accusations and said that the Jews' guilt should be proved 'By the judgement of God', and called upon them to face trial by ordeal, and the bishop took a firmer stance by repeating Godwine's summons and added that 'unless they came immediately to purge themselves they must understand that without doubt they would be exterminated'.

In fear of their lives, the Jews appealed to the Sheriff for help and protection from the angry mob. As the King's representative the Sheriff had no choice other than to comply with their appeal, and offered the entire Jewish community of Norwich refuge in the castle where they would be safe behind its stone walls.

They eagerly took up the offer, and remained in the castle until Bishop Eborard, not wishing to come into open conflict with the Sheriff or the King, and the case being unproven, dismissed the Synod, thus quietening the disgruntled Godwine and his supporters.

A SAINT IN THE MAKING

The matter of the murdered boy William might well have ended when the Jews were free from fear of attack and able to return to their habitats and resume normal living conditions.

But Aymar, Prior of St. Pancras at Lewes in Sussex, who as an owner of large estates in the Norwich diocese had attended the Synod, was convinced that Godwine's accusations were true.

He also saw the possibilities of political and financial gain for his Priory in Lewes if it possessed the body of a boy martyred by Jews, and sought the permission of Bishop Eborard to exhume it from the grave in Thorpe Wood and convey it to Lewes.

After careful thought, Bishop Eborard decided that if William was to be venerated as a martyr the church of Norwich ought to reap the benefit, and refused Prior Aymar permission to exhume the body, but promptly arranged its exhumation himself. Consequently, William's little body was dug up and carried on a bier into Norwich Cathedral.

There were no signs of corruption on the body, but it is said to have had clear marks on its hands and feet as evidence of crucifixion, and William was therefore acknowledged as a martyr.

The body was carefully washed and prepared for re-burial in the monk's cemetery. But interest in the 'martyred' boy was minimal and waned further until 1146 when Bishop Eborard retired to the Abbey of Fontenay in France. Word spread that William Turbe, Prior of Norwich, was favoured to replace Eborard.

Sheriff John de Chesney was disturbed by the news of the bishop's retirement and that the Jew-hating William Turbe was the most likely candidate to succeed him.

In spite of suffering from an internal haemorrhage, John journeyed to London in an attempt to prevent Turbe being elected, but his mission was in vain and Turbe was duly elected Bishop of Norwich.

Aggrieved at having failed in his mission, John returned to Norfolk, carried in a litter, weak and barely conscious. His servants managed to convey him as far as his manor house at Mileham, where, too ill to continue, he died soon after arriving. His brother, William de Chesney, succeeded him as Sheriff of Norfolk and Suffolk.

Turbe had risen to his position from humble birth, and had grown to hate the Jewish money-lenders. He believed them to be responsible for the boy William's death, and like his predecessor, was well aware that Norwich possessed no crowd-pulling relics, and would benefit greatly if the murdered boy were to be made a patron saint of Norwich Cathedral.

Thus he had the body of William removed from the monks' cemetery and transferred to a new tomb in the Chapter House with due pomp and ceremony, and the people of Norwich began to venerate William as a saint. Word quickly spread throughout the region, and it was not long before pilgrims from all over East Anglia began visiting the tomb.

Soon, so-called 'miracles' were attributed to William, and his Shrine at Norwich attracted thousands of pilgrims from all over the country.

The Bishop of Norwich had succeeded in his quest to provide a substantial new source of income from the offerings which pilgrims generously deposited in the donation box, strategically placed next to the Shrine.

A LULL IN HOSTILITIES

In the tenth year of Stephen's turbulent reign, both sides were weary of the civil war, and the common people, who had suffered most, yearned for peace. According to one chronicler. 'the King's fortunes began to change for the better'.

Although devastated by the anarchy and tyranny of the local barons, calm finally settled over East Anglia, for, after ten years of civil strife, even the barons had had enough.

Having put down de Manderville's rebellion and made peace with Hugh Bigod, who seemed content to retire to his castle at Bungay and devote his time to restoring his neglected estates, King Stephen was able to spend more time on matters of state, and on rebuilding the shattered economy.

Hugh Bigod still had designs on regaining the constableship of Norwich Castle, but was prepared to bide his time, meanwhile building a new and bigger castle than the one at Bungay at nearby Framlingham.

But King Stephen was not happy to reinstate Nigel le Poer as Bishop of Ely when the rebellious Nigel returned to England from Rome with letters from the Pope confirming his position. The letters also stipulated that all liberties and possessions of the Church of Ely were to be restored to him.

Stephen felt reluctant to acknowledge Nigel as Bishop of Ely after he had rebelled against him, but, after the nobles of his court pointed out that it would antagonise the Pope, he reluctantly permitted Nigel to return to his diocese on condition that he paid a fine of 300 marks.

Nigel promised to pay the fine, but was shocked when he returned to Ely and discovered the area impoverished, the church looted and in great disorder after being occupied by de Manderville's soldiers.

There was no money or treasures left in the cathedral's treasury. The only means left to him in order to pay the fine was to strip the Shrine of St. Etheldreda of its silver. The fine paid, Bishop Nigel now weary of political intrigue, settled down to the clerical duties of his diocese.

The Empress Maud suffered a major set-back on the 31st October 1147 when her half-brother Robert, Earl of Gloucester, suddenly died. She found it difficult to maintain her position after the loss of the commander of her soldiers, so departed for Anjou a few weeks after Robert's death and never returned to England again.

THE SECOND CRUSADE

When news reached the West in 1144 that the Christian city of Edessa in Syria had been captured by the Saracens, the Pope immediately called for action. He authorised Bernard, Abbot of Clairvaux, to preach and recruit volunteers for a crusade against the infidels.

At Vezelay in France, Bernard preached a rousing sermon to an immense gathering of people and promised that everyone who took part in the crusade would receive full remission of their sins. Louis the Young, King of France, was so impressed by Bernard's sermon, he promised to raise and lead an army to Syria and free Edessa from the infidels. William de Warenne, Earl of Surrey, who was amongst the crowd at Vezelay, was also influenced by Bernard's appeal, and promised to join King Louis' army.

It took King Louis three years to raise money to equip an army consisting of 70,000 horsemen. The vast army, with King Louis at its head, set off from St Denis on its long trek to the Holy Land in June 1147.

They crossed Europe via Germany, Austria, Hungary, then through the Balkans, and eventually arrived in Constantinople on 4th October 1147. There King Louis and his barons were sumptuously entertained at the Imperial Palace by the Emperor Manual Comnenus, and given sight-seeing tours of the ancient city.

After a few weeks of luxurious living and rest, the army set off to cross Asia Minor. They were hampered by winter storms, freezing nights, precipitous mountains, deep gorges and swollen rivers, and were constantly harassed by attacks from the Turks.

On leaving the town of Laodicea one morning in early January 1148, the army had difficulty in ascending a high mountain. Whilst the main part of the army crossed the mountain, King Louis assigned William de Warenne and a contingent of knights to protect the rear of the army and the baggage. The

Turks attacked in force, taking the rear guard by surprise. Confused by the unexpected attack and surrounded on all sides, Earl William was slain and his knights annihilated.

"On that day," lamented one chronicler, "fell the valour of the French."

After further disasters and futile attempts to re-capture Edessa, King Louis and his remaining army returned home in humiliating defeat.

THE WARENNE SUCCESSION

The death of Earl William de Warenne left the de Warenne family without a male heir, consequently, his only daughter, Isabella, succeeded him as Countess of Surrey and inherited the family estates.

No doubt there were many suitors who sought the hand in marriage of such a wealthy heiress, but Isabella's mother, the Countess Ela, had the final say on whom her daughter should marry.

Ela favoured King Stephen's younger son, William de Blois, as a suitable husband for her daughter, and arranged a prestigious marriage between them within months of her husband's death.

William de Blois was already Lord of Norwich, and as Lord of the Honour of Eye, a major landowner in Norfolk, Suffolk and Lincolnshire, with the greatest of his domains at Eye where his great castle dominated the landscape.

After his marriage to Isabella, William adopted the title Earl de Warenne and took control of his wife's vast estates, including command of the castles at Acre in Norfolk, Lewes in Sussex, Reigate in Surrey and Conisbrough in Yorkshire.

William de Blois, Earl de Warenne, thus became one of the richest and most powerful barons in England, much to the annoyance of Hugh Bigod, who had long been hostile to King Stephen and his family for ousting him from the position of Constable of Norwich.

Hugh Bigod saw Earl William as a rival for power in the East of England, and King Stephen considered crushing the power of Bigod by depriving him of the Earldom of Norfolk and giving it to William.

But the rivalry and tension between the two Earls threatened the peace of the region, and the King decided it would be unwise to antagonise Bigod further and allowed him to retain his Earldom.

DEATH OF THE QUEEN

Aubrey the Grim, Earl of Oxford, who had supported and received his title from Empress Maud, when she was briefly in power, made his peace with King Stephen when the Empress left England, and he became a good and loyal friend to Stephen and Queen Matilda. Consequently the King allowed Aubrey to retain his title and keep his lands.

Queen Matilda died at Hedingham Castle, the fortified home of Aubrey the Grim. – *EARLY TWENTIETH CENTURY POSTCARD.*

The long years of war and struggle had wearied Queen Matilda, and the comparative quiet caused her to think seriously about her true purpose in life. After long consideration, she came to the conclusion that she should devote her time to works of charity and benevolence.

She established hospitals, built churches and founded an abbey at Faversham in Kent, then took up residence in a Canterbury nunnery so that she could supervise the building of the abbey, as it was her wish to be buried in the abbey's church when she died.

By 1151 the construction at Faversham was nearing completion, and Matilda decided to leave the nunnery to tour her estates in East Anglia. While she was in the region she was invited to stay at Hedingham Castle by Aubrey the Grim.

After only a few day's stay, she fell ill with a fever. Weak and exhausted, Queen Matilda died on the 3rd May 1151. She was only forty-seven years old and, according to her wishes, was buried in Faversham Abbey Church.

One chronicler of the time was so impressed by Queen Matilda's benevolence that he was moved to write, 'if ever a woman deserved to be carried by the hand of Angels to Heaven, it was this holy woman'.

THE VENGEANCE OF ST. EDMUND

Matilda's death so early in life brought home to the grieving King Stephen his own mortality and that he ought to secure the succession of the throne for Eustace, his eldest son, and ensure the continuation of the House of Blois.

After deliberation he decided that Eustace should be crowned King while he still lived, thus hopefully ensuring a smooth and unrivalled succession when the time came, and sent communication to the Pope for approval of his intention. Eustace, however, was a man of few morals 'who was fond of low company', and had little respect for the church. The Pope, no doubt being advised of the ungodly reputation of Eustace by the English bishops, who had no desire to see him crowned king, refused to give authority for his coronation and forbade Archbishop Theobald of Canterbury to perform the ceremony.

Undeterred by the Pope's decision, King Stephen ordered Archbishop Theobald to crown Eustace King, but Theobald, who secretly favoured the Angevin cause, flatly refused.

His refusal so angered Stephen that he had the Archbishop thrown into prison, and confiscated all his lands and wealth. But Theobald managed to escape from confinement and fled across the Channel to Flanders with the help of sympathisers.

Early in 1153 Henry of Anjou, the son of Empress Maud, took advantage of the controversy surrounding succession to the throne, and landed in England with a large army intent on doing battle with King Stephen.

Stephen mustered his reluctant forces and the two rivals met to engage in combat at Wallingford, Oxfordshire. But the barons, tired of perpetual war, intervened, and pressed the King to call a truce and negotiate a settlement with Henry before further senseless slaughter commenced.

Having lost the support of the barons. King Stephen had little choice but to sign a Treaty with Henry, acknowledging him as his heir to the throne of England and granting him the Duchy of Normandy.

Satisfied that he would one day be King of England, Henry withdrew his forces and returned to Normandy. Eustace, however, was furious at the loss of what he considered was his rightful inheritance, and mustered his army of supporters with intent to vent his anger.

He took them on the rampage through Cambridgeshire and into Suffolk, ordering his men 'to set fire to houses everywhere', and 'to kill those who came in the way', burning and pillaging indiscriminately until he reached Bury St. Edmunds.

Seeing such a large force of soldiers at the gates of Bury Abbey, the Abbot tried to placate Eustace by receiving and entertaining him in the abbey. Eustace gladly accepted the Abbot's invitation, but having taken advantage of his hospitality, demanded a ransom so that he could pay his soldiers.

The Abbot, offended by the ingratitude of Eustace after he having been welcomed to the abbey and wined and dined sumptuously, found the courage to refuse his demand.

Eustace infuriated by the Abbot's refusal, stormed out of the abbey and with his soldiers set about plundering the surrounding villages that belonged to the abbey, burning their crops.

A week later, on the 17th August 1153, Eustace was suddenly struck by severe pains when he was eating a meal. The pains increased and became unbearable until he finally collapsed and died.

A chronicler claimed that his premature death was due to the vengeance of St. Edmund for the destruction he had caused to the abbey's estates. Nevertheless, his irreligious life either forgiven or forgotten, Eustace was laid to rest beside his mother, Queen Matilda, in the church of Faversham Abbey.

The following year King Stephen, worn out and weary, died of a heart attack on 25th October 1154. His body was also taken to Faversham where it was laid to rest next to his beloved wife.

So ended the House of Blois.

CHAPTER FIVE

The Angevin Ascendancy, 1154–1185

THE RECALL OF BISHOP NIGEL

Henry of Anjou was in Normandy when news of King Stephen's death reached him. He was delayed from crossing the Channel for six weeks, due to violent weather. Eventually, when he arrived in England on 7th December 1154, he was crowned King of England in Westminster Abbey twelve days later by Archbishop Theobald.

Although only 21 years old, Henry II was the complete opposite in character to his predecessor. Strong-willed, like his mother, the Empress Maud, he had a fiery temper, was intelligent, energetic, and keen to restore order to his kingdom after it had undergone almost 20 years of civil war.

During those long, turbulent years, the Treasury of England was in such disarray that it had practically ceased to function. The county sheriffs, who were responsible for collecting taxes, had either failed to do so, or had kept the majority of the amounts they had collected for their personal gain, surrendering only a small portion to the Treasury.

Disturbed by this state of affairs, the new King made it a priority to re-organise the Treasury, and called upon Nigel, Bishop of Ely, who had unrivalled knowledge of running the Treasury, having acted as Treasurer during the latter years of Henry I's and the early years of King Stephen's reign, to take on the task again.

Nigel was reluctant to return to government office at first, preferring to spend his days administering his diocese, but eventually gave in to the King's persistent appeals, and returned to Court to take up his old position as Head of the Exchequer.

Faced with the formidable task of re-organising the national income, Nigel began by revising the system of recording accounts, ensuring that they were orderly and accurate, also auditing the sheriffs annual returns to make sure they brought in all the income due.

By 1157 the systematic workings of the Treasury had almost recovered, thanks to the efforts of Bishop Nigel. The amount of revenue brought in by the county sheriffs had doubled, and Nigel moved the Exchequer, which had been attached to the King's itinerant court, to a permanent base in Westminster.

THE HONEST SHERIFF OF CAMBRIDGESHIRE
The Sheriff of each county represented royal authority, and was responsible for organising the collection of taxes, fines, rents and other amounts due to the Treasury.

King Henry was determined to re-establish the authority of the monarchy by bringing the sheriffs into check, and dismissed those who had been dishonest during the long years of anarchy and replaced them with his loyal minions.

Pain de Hemmingford, who had been made Sheriff of Cambridgeshire and Huntingdon by King Stephen in 1139, was one of the few who were considered trustworthy by Henry, he was confirmed in his position and, in addition, given the Shrievalty of Surrey.

After many years of pillage and plunder, the town of Cambridge was in a ruinous condition, twice being attacked and burnt during the anarchy. Likewise, the surrounding lands and villages in the county had also been despoiled.

The local economy was in such a desperate state that Pain obviously had difficulty in extracting taxes from the impoverished inhabitants. Nevertheless, he managed to gather all he could from the people to replenish the dwindling coffers of the Treasury.

In 1156 he set off for Westminster with chests full of silver coins, slung across the backs of pack horses, protected by an escort of armed soldiers. Outlaws still roamed the countryside, and Pain was all too aware that if he lost the tax money he would be at the 'King's mercy'.

Pain and his entourage arrived safely in London and handed over his returns, which were counted on the great table of the Exchequer, so-called from the black and white chequered table cloth, which was used as a reckoner to calculate the moneys brought in by the sheriffs.

Pain's honesty was rewarded. An amount of £4 was returned to him to be used to assist the ruined town and county of Cambridge to recover.

THE COUNCIL OF BURY ST. EDMUNDS
Having established a stable government of loyal and trusted servants, Henry II turned his attention to the powerful barons whose unruly behaviour had contributed to the years of anarchy during the reign of his predecessor.

One of the most troublesome barons was Hugh Bigod, Earl of Norfolk, who had built up a strong power-base in East Anglia. His ambition to become the most powerful baron in the region, however, had long been thwarted by William de Blois, Earl of Surrey, son of the late King Stephen.

William had acquired large land holdings in Norfolk and Suffolk, and controlled the important castles of Norwich, Eye and Acre. Bigod had no love for the House of Blois, and William had nothing but contempt for the two-faced treacherous Bigod.

Bitter rivalry had long existed between the two nobles, and, as tension mounted, King Henry decided it was time to show who had overall authority in East Anglia before their quest for power led to hostilities.

Henry summoned a Great Council of the Realm to meet at Bury St. Edmunds on 19th May 1157, and arrived at Bury with a vast retinue of court officials and a large army of knights and soldiers. This impressive

King Henry II called a Great Council of the Realm to meet at Bury St. Edmunds.

show of strength was a demonstration to the local barons that any disloyalty or rejection of his authority would not be tolerated.

Bigod was shocked and angered when he was summoned before the King and ordered to surrender his castles at Bungay, Framlingham and Walton to the crown. A small consolation was that he was permitted to retain his title of Earl of Norfolk, but with his castles in the hands of the King, he had been virtually stripped of his power.

Although William de Blois was the late King Stephen's son, he posed no threat to the crown. Nevertheless, Henry decided that he should also be stripped of some of his power. He therefore deprived him of the Castle and Constableship of Norwich and the Honour and Castle of Eye in Suffolk.

King Henry appointed constables to act as custodians of Bigod's castles, and William de Chesney, the Sheriff of Norfolk was granted custody of Norwich Castle.

The Honour and Castle of Eye was placed in the custody of Thomas Beckett, Chancellor, friend and confessor of the King, who eventually became Archbishop of Canterbury.

So ended the meeting of the Great Council at Bury St. Edmunds. In crushing the friction between the most powerful barons in East Anglia, King Henry was convinced that he had prevented the outbreak of civil war.

THE LECHEROUS LORD OF RAYLEIGH

Henry de Essex, Lord of Rayleigh and grandson of Sweyn the Great Sheepmaster, fared well under the new monarch, who recognised his hereditary right to the office of Standard-Bearer of England, and also made him Sheriff of Bedfordshire.

Whether the neighbouring de Vere family was aware of the lecherous and ill reputation of Henry de Essex or not is unknown, but Aubrey the Grim willingly gave his sister, Adeliza, in marriage to de Essex. This advantageous union with the House of de Vere brought to Henry de Essex respectability and social advancement.

The marriage was unhappy from the start, for in spite of his incessant sexual demands, Adeliza was unable to bear him children. Henry's outbursts of violent anger towards her because of her inability to provide him with an heir caused her to seek solace in the arms of a knight named Gilbert.

When de Essex found out that his wife was being unfaithful he flew into a violent rage. To save herself from physical attack, Adelita unkindly blamed Gilbert for her indiscretions, saying that she had been 'unable to withstand his passionate demands'.

Henry de Essex immediately imprisoned Gilbert in his castle at Rayleigh, and had him tortured to death.

A vile, merciless and selfish man, de Essex claimed that everything and everyone on his estates were subject to his rules and whims, and no-one under his authority escaped his extortionate rent demands. He even alienated the Abbot of Bury St. Edmunds by refusing to pay rents on lands he held on the abbey's estates. No matter what threats and demands the Abbot made, Henry refused to hand over the money, keeping it for himself.

He was also feared by his tenants for frequently roaming his estates in search of young maidens to seduce. On one such occasion he visited the house of tenant Roger Kirtley in the Manor of Mutford, near Lowestoft, and demanded his young daughter, claiming Kirtley had promised her to him.

Kirtley, having changed his mind, objected and would not surrender his daughter to him, refusing de Essex entry into his house. Infuriated by Kirtley's stubborn resistance, de Essex broke down the door and searched the house for the young woman, but could not find her.

Suspecting that she had escaped through a bedroom window, he went outside and searched the barn, which was full of harvest corn, but she was not to be found there either, and Kirtley refused to disclose the location of her hiding place.

Henry de Essex flew into a raging temper and set fire to the barn, destroying the building, leaving poor Kirtley in despair at losing his valuable crop of corn, but satisfied that he had saved his daughter's virginity.

THE STANDARD-BEARER'S DISGRACE

Lord Rayleigh's tenants had an unexpected respite from his lecherous roaming in 1157 when the King called upon his services as Standard-Bearer of England. Henry II had decided to mount a military expedition to quell the ambitious Welsh Chieftain, Owen of Gwynedd, whose aim was to establish his own supreme authority over the Welsh.

The King gathered a large force of knights from all over the realm, including contingents from East Anglia, led by Henry de Essex, the Standard-Bearer, and Roger de Clare, Earl of Hertford.

Reinforced by archers from Shropshire, the army assembled at Chester, and crossed the River Dee into Wales in the early summer of 1157.

King Henry's intention was to follow the coastal route through north Wales and attack Owen at Rhuddlan, but on reaching Colehill he decided to take a small force of highly armed knights through the Forrest of Cennadlog with the intention of making a surprise attack on Rhuddlan.

The decision proved disastrous, for, while passing through a valley in the forest the small force was ambushed by the Welsh. The King's forces, taken completely by surprise, were thrown into confusion and suffered heavy losses, and word quickly spread that the King had been slain.

Convinced that the King was dead, Henry de Essex, threw down the Royal Standard and shouted in a loud voice that the King was dead as he fled from the scene of battle, causing panic among the remaining knights, who began to retreat.

But the King was not dead, although he had been wounded in the skirmish, and it was only by the prompt action of Roger de Clare that he was rescued from the chaos and carried to a safe place.

Roger then picked up the Royal Standard and encouraged the scattered knights to reform and retreat in ignominious defeat and rejoin the main army.

Although Henry's expedition against the Welsh had ended disastrously, Owen of Gwynedd knew that Henry of England fully intended to bring northern Wales under his control. To give himself time to consolidate his position in readiness for the next attack, Owen agreed to cede the territory between the River Dee and Rhuddlan to King Henry.

THE DUEL

Although Henry de Essex had disgraced himself on the field of battle by flinging down the Royal Standard and fleeing, the King saw no reason to bring charges of treachery against him.

But a certain knight, named Robert de Montfort, who had been there at the time, persistently accused Henry of cowardice and treachery. The accusations and jibes went on for several years, until the two agreed to settle the issue by a judicial duel in the presence of the King.

Fry's island on the Thames at Caversham, near Reading, was chosen as the most suitable site for the duel, and the combatants met there in March 1163. The contest attracted a great crowd of people to watch and see the outcome.

When the combat began it was soon obvious that Henry was no match for the younger Robert de Montfort, who quickly gained the upper hand by raining savage blows on Henry, who nevertheless fought back courageously until his strength began to fail.

He then supposedly saw a vision of St. Edmund floating in mid-air above the river. The Saint looked angry and began to shake his head at Henry as if he was reprimanding him for his wicked ways. Henry, already weakened by his opponents onslaught, fell to the ground, his body hacked by savage wounds.

At the request of his relatives, the monks of Reading Abbey took possession of his body and began to prepare it for burial in the abbey when they discovered he was still alive. After careful nursing he recovered, but maimed and disgraced, his castle and estates seized by the King, Henry de Essex took the monastic habit and chose to live out the remainder of his life in Reading Abbey.

According to one chronicler he did so 'to cleanse the stain of his earlier days'.

THE END OF THE HOUSE OF BLOIS

In 1159 the barons and knights of the realm were summoned by the King to join a military expedition to Toulouse. He claimed that the French County of Toulouse was part of his wife's inheritance, and demanded that the present usurper surrender it to the rightful heir, Eleanor of Aquitaine.

King Louis the Young, of France, who was overlord of Toulouse, disputed the claim, and objected to the county being added to the English King's domains. Hence King Henry decided to seize Toulouse by force.

Many of the barons and knights of England were reluctant to join the expedition, and instead of actively taking part themselves opted to pay scutage, a tax which enabled the King to hire mercenaries.

One East Anglian baron who chose to lead his own soldiers was William de

Blois, the Earl Warenne, youngest son of the late King Stephen, who remained loyal to King Henry, despite losing his lordships of Norwich and Eye.

William was still one of the wealthiest barons in England, holding the considerable Honour of Warenne, by right of his marriage to Countess Isabella de Warenne, and was therefore able to muster a sizeable contingent of knights and soldiers.

In his own right as Count of Boulogne, he controlled the French port of Wissant and accumulated more wealth from continental trade from England, much of which must have been wool shorn from the sheep pastured on his own extensive Essex and Sussex lands.

William de Blois, Lord of Norwich, and first husband of Isabella de Warenne.

William gathered his soldiers and joined the King's forces at Dover. It was the largest army assembled since the First Crusade, and was transported across the Channel in a fleet of forty-five vessels.

The huge army trekked across the continental domains of King Henry to the County of Toulouse, capturing the town of Cahors, with little resistance.

When the King's army reached the City of Toulouse in July they found it occupied by King Louis, and encamped outside the city walls. Henry was reluctant to alienate King Louis and throughout the summer attempted to negotiate amicable terms with the French monarch.

While the two Kings deliberated over a peaceful settlement, a fatal fever spread through the camp of the English army. Many died of the sickness, including William de Blois.

Henry made no headway in his talks with King Louis, and had little choice but to withdraw his considerably depleted army from Toulouse and return to England, the whole venture being a costly failure.

ISABELLA'S SECOND MARRIAGE

The widowed Countess Isabella de Warenne attracted several suitors in the years following the death of her husband, William de Blois. Their marriage had been childless, and it was therefore important that she re-marry and produce an heir who would succeed to the family estates. Isabella was sought after by the noble families of England as a bride for one of their sons, but she remained unmarried until 1164.

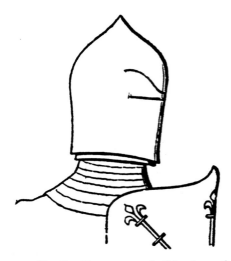

Hamlin Plantagenet, half-brother of King Henry II, and second husband of Isabella de Warenne.

King Henry saw the advantage of uniting the wealth and power of the de Warennes with the Royal House, and arranged a marriage between Isabella and his illegitimate half-brother, Hamelin Plantagenet.

Although illegitimate, Hamelin was an acknowledged son of Geoffrey of Anjou, and was educated in the art of combat, the same as legitimate male members of his family.

Geoffrey's family was said to have been descended from the daughter of Satan, because they were all renowned for their cruel temperament. All his male offspring excelled in shedding blood, either in war or hunting.

Hamelin was known by the name of Plantagenet, a name acquired from his father's habit of always wearing a sprig of the broom plant, 'Planta Genet', in his hat.

On his marriage to Isabella, however, Hamelin adopted the name and title of Earl Warenne, content to preside over his wife's domains in the lavish style befitting any member of the Royal Family, and remained a loyal supporter of his half-brother, King Henry.

THE BANKRUPT SHERIFF

When King Henry II succeeded to the throne, he dismissed William de Chesney from the office of Sheriff of Norfolk. William had been appointed by King Stephen and, although he had not taken an active part in the civil war, he had remained loyal to Stephen throughout his troublesome reign.

King Henry therefore mistrusted him and dismissed him from office, replacing him with one of his loyal minions. But two years later, when the office fell vacant William de Chesney having regained favour with the King, managed to purchase the office of Sheriff as well as regaining the custody of Norwich Castle.

William had borrowed heavily from the Jewish money-lenders of Norwich to raise the purchase price of the Sheriffdom, expecting that the collected taxes and rents would not only meet the King's annual demand, but would yield a profit for himself thus enabling him to gradually pay off his debts.

He had not taken into account that the King would increase the amount of tax annually, forcing William to extract more money from the tax payers of the county, in the vain hope that the surplus would continue flowing in.

But the higher the taxes and rents were fixed, the more difficult it was for William to collect them, and by 1163 his debts to the money-lenders had increased to £460. His tax returns also showed a serious deficit to the Exchequer of £200.

King Henry decided that William de Chesney's financial situation was unacceptable and dismissed him from office until he had repaid all his debts, replacing him with one of his Royal Stewards, Ogga the Dapifer, who assumed the responsibilities of Sheriff, except custody of Norwich Castle, which the King entrusted to Hugh Bigod, Earl of Norfolk. Bigod had led a settled life and taken no part in politics since Henry's accession to the throne. The King must therefore have considered the 70 year old warrior harmless to have entrusted him with the care of such an important Royal castle.

William de Chesney struggled to pay off his debts for the rest of his life. When he died in 1174, William still owed the Exchequer £190. It is not known what he owed the moneylenders, but the King insisted that Margaret, William de Chesney's only daughter and heir, became responsible for his debt to the Exchequer.

Within two years the astute Margaret had successfully paid off all her father's debts, with the exception of £19 owed to the Exchequer, which the King pardoned.

A NEW ROYAL CASTLE

On 26th January 1165 a severe earth tremor rocked the counties of Norfolk, Suffolk and Cambridgeshire – throwing people to the ground and causing considerable structural damage to buildings. According to one chronicler. 'the church bells began ringing, such was the force of the tremor'.

In general, the people of East Anglia had little cause to welcome the New Year, for they had to set about repairing the damage to the churches, monasteries and houses. But there were exceptions, notably Hugh Bigod, for whom things could not have been better. The cunning old Earl had gradually regained the favour of the King, who thought that Bigod had mellowed and could be trusted in old age.

He consequently returned the castles of Bungay and Framlingham to him upon payment of a £1000 fine, but also considered it prudent to construct a new castle in the heart of Bigod's Suffolk territory at Orford, not just to ensure Bigod remained loyal, but to protect the East Coast from foreign invasion.

Ogga, the Sheriff of Norfolk and Suffolk, was appointed to superintend the building of the new castle, ably assisted by William the Chaplain, who was also given the responsibility of erecting a new church at Orford.

Orford Castle, constructed for Henry II, in the heart of Bigod's territory.

In addition to ordering the construction of a castle and church at Orford, the King also instructed that the harbour of the town was to be enlarged and deepened so that larger vessels could berth.

During the first year of construction of the castle, £660 was expended on a large quantity of stone transported from Caen, France, and timber brought from the forests of Yorkshire. The bulk of the cost came from the profits of the Royal Manors, the balance from taxation.

The work progressed so rapidly that the castle keep had been almost completed by the end of the year.

THE WILD MAN

By the end of the second year, the keep and part of the curtain walls of Orford Castle were sufficiently complete to enable the King to garrison the building and appoint a constable.

He chose Bartholomew de Glanville, Lord of Bacton in Norfolk, a trusted knight with an exemplary record, to take up the position, which also entailed overseeing the remaining construction work to complete the curtain walls, towers and gatehouse.

Bartholomew was well-chosen for his position. The Glanville family had acquired the Lordship of Bacton during the reign of William Rufus, and

Bartholomew's father, William, founded a priory for Cluniac monks at nearby Bromeholm in 1113.

When his father died Bartholomew inherited the Lordship of Bacton, and magnanimously endowed the Priory with the church of Bacton, and those of Dilham, Keswick and Paston, together with the tithes of several surrounding parishes.

During the early days of Bartholomew's appointment as Constable, a strange event occurred. Some Orford fishermen casting their nets off Boyton, caught what they first thought to be a large fish, but upon dragging in their nets found it to be what was later described by a chronicler as a 'Wild Man'.

The man was alive, naked and completely covered with hair, including a long shaggy beard. When questioned as to who he was and what he was doing in the sea, he replied in an incomprehensible language. Mystified by their catch the fishermen took him to Orford Castle to appear before Bartholomew de Glanville.

Bartholomew, frustrated by not getting a sensible reply from the strange man, had him hung up by the legs and flogged, to get some sense out of him, but to no avail. He was taken down, and kept in the castle dungeon and guarded day and night to prevent him escaping and returning to the sea.

The strange man was of regular habits, going to bed at sunset and rising with the morning sun, ate whatever food was given to him, but was particularly partial to fish, whether cooked or raw.

Apart from remaining incomprehensible in speech he was no trouble, so one day his warders decided to take him to the estuary of the river and let him have a swim.

They hung nets on all sides to hedge him in, but after enjoying a surface swim, the Wild Man unexpectedly dived deep, swam under the nets and escaped into the open sea.

Bartholomew de Glanville was astonished when he turned up at the castle gates a few days later as though nothing had happened, giving his usual gibberish explanation.

He stayed in an unguarded dungeon for two months, then must have decided that he'd had enough of land life and calmly walked out, presumably returning to the sea for he was never seen again. Who he was, and from where he came, remains a mystery.

THE PASSING OF BISHOP NIGEL

Bishop Nigel of Ely had held the office of state Treasurer since 1126, except for a short time during the reign of King Stephen. He was never really dedicated to the church, spending most of his time on matters of state, particularly in the financial affairs of the realm.

Due to his skill and expertise, the Exchequer was restored to the efficiency that existed during the reign of King Henry I. Nigel accomplished this by establishing a permanent base in Westminster, and introducing biannual audits of the county sheriffs' accounts to ensure all their dues had been paid to the Exchequer.

In 1164 the old bishop suffered a stroke, which left him partially paralysed, and he was unable to continue the demanding role of Treasurer, but secured the position for his son, Richard FitzNigel by paying the King 1000 marks.

Nigel returned to Ely, where he lived in peaceful retirement until his death on Friday, 30th May 1169. His funeral was conducted by William Turbe, Bishop of Norwich, on the following Sunday, and he was laid to rest near the altar of the Holy Cross in Ely Cathedral.

Richard, the son of Nigel's mistress, was an intelligent and wise man. During his youth he was educated at the monastery of Ely and later served his father well as a Clerk of the Exchequer, where he received training in the kingdom's accounting system and all matters relating to the running of the Exchequer.

When he succeeded his father as Treasurer he continued to improve the work begun by his father in reorganising the Exchequer to maximise efficiency, and so successful was he that he held the office for the next thirty-four years.

REBELLION OF THE KING'S SON

To help govern his vast empire more effectively, King Henry had given his domains on the continent to his sons to rule, but had restricted their authority. He still held the reins of power, and retained most of the income gathered from the territories, much to the dissatisfaction of his power-hungry and unruly offspring.

His eldest son, also named Henry, was a weak and selfish young man of unstable temperament. He was particularly aggrieved by his father's unwillingness to entrust him with more power, and the constant quarrels between them eventually turned into open rebellion.

Young Henry, supported by his mother, Queen Eleanor, who had lived on the continent apart from her estranged husband for several years, raised a huge army, mainly consisting of Flemish mercenaries, under the command of the Earl of Leicester, with the intention of invading England.

THE EARL OF LEICESTER'S WAR

Robert Blanchmain, Earl of Leicester, accompanied by his wife, Countess Petronilla, landed on the Suffolk coast at Walton on 29th September 1173 with an army of 3000 Flemings. Encountering no resistance, he led his army inland to Framlingham Castle, where he was sure they would receive hospitality and support from Hugh Bigod.

The 80-year-old Earl of Norfolk had been lying low for several years, but welcomed the chance at striking a blow against Royal authority, and the Earl of Leicester's arrival at Framlingham prompted him to throw in his lot with the rebels.

Whilst entertaining the Earl and Countess, Bigod began mobilising his forces, and the two men spent time plotting their strategy. They decided that their first action should be to capture and gain control of the important town and port of Dunwich.

Their combined forces plundered and pillaged their way to Dunwich, but the Burgesses of the town, having had prior warning of their approach, had closed the heavy town gates, preventing entry. The Burgesses had also organised a local militia to resist attack.

Frustrated by being brought to an unexpected halt the two Earls issued an ultimatum to the Burgesses to the effect that either they surrender the town, or that no townsman would escape death or injury.

The Earl of Leicester even began to erect gallows outside the town walls, on which he threatened to hang the Burgesses when he had captured the town.

Undeterred by his threats, the Burgesses had the support of all the people of Dunwich, who were determined to defend the town. Consequently, every able-bodied man was called upon to man the ramparts to repel the besiegers by hurling whatever missiles they could lay their hands on.

Even the women played a part by collecting stones and carrying them to the men, who hurled them down on to the besiegers, and time after time the rebels were repelled by the defiant townsfolk.

The town was so well defended that the Earl of Leicester eventually withdrew his forces, concluding that the town could not be taken without a lengthy siege and, perhaps at the suggestion of Bigod, they marched west with the intention of seizing the Royal Castle of Haughley, which lay halfway between Ipswich and Bury.

THE FALL OF HAUGHLEY CASTLE

The castle at Haughley was originally built by the de Montfort family after the Norman Conquest, but had escheated to the Crown during the reign of King Stephen.

It was of large proportions and constructed mainly of wood in the motto and bailey style. The keep was atop a massive mound, about 80 feet high, surrounded by a water-filled ditch, and the vast outer bailey, enclosed by earthworks topped with a wooden palisade, stretched 100 yards to the south.

Ralph de Broc, an adventurer knight who had supported the King in his

Hugh Bigod was defeated by the Royalists in a ferocious battle at Fornham All Saints.

dispute with Archbishop Becket and had administered the diocese of Canterbury during the Archbishops exile, was in command of the impressive castle, having been appointed Constable of Haughley by the King in 1170 after playing a minor part in Becket's murder.

But in spite of its size and formidable appearance, the castle was only garrisoned by about 30 men, who stood little chance of defending it against the combined forces of the two Earls, who easily breached the walls upon their arrival at the castle.

As the Flemings poured into the outer bailey, Ralph de Broc and his soldiers retreated to the keep, where they gallantly resisted the onslaught of the Flemings, who sustained many casualties as they crossed the moat carrying brushwood, and climbed up the mound to reach the keep.

Heedless of high casualties, the Flemings piled the brushwood against the wooden walls of the keep and set fire to it, then retreated to watch the keep burn.

Ralph de Broc and his small force hastily fled from the blazing keep to avoid being roasted alive, and surrendered. Ralph was taken prisoner to be held to ransom, while the remainder of his small garrison were put to the sword in a bloody slaughter and their bodies thrown into a burial pit.

The jubilant Earls, having accomplished their mission, returned to Framlingham Castle, leaving Haughley a smouldering ruin.

THE BATTLE OF FORNHAM ALL SAINTS

The two Earls arrived back at Framlingham Castle to find the domestic situation in chaos. Bigod had left the smooth-running of routine daily affairs in the hands of his wife, the Countess Gundrada, but the Countess Petronilla of Leicester, whose tempestuous nature was renowned, interfered, disagreed and argued about almost everything, until the domestic running of the castle was in complete disarray.

Robert Blanchmain and Hugh Bigod were concerned that the bitter quarrel between their wives would threaten the alliance formed between them. The Earl of Leicester, therefore, agreed to leave the castle and continue with his original plan, taking his belligerent wife with him.

Blanchmain planned to capture the town of Leicester and then link up with the Earl of Chester's rebel army in the North, with Bigod accompanying him as far as Cambridge, which they planned to capture and plunder.

Meanwhile, Richard de Lucy, Chief Justiciar of England and virtual regent while the King was on the Continent dealing with his unruly son, received news of the rebellion and gathered an army.

Lucy marched into East Anglia, where he was joined by a force led by Hamelin, Earl Warenne. and a contingent of knights sent by the Abbot of Bury St Edmunds, who brought the precious Standard of St. Edmund with them, having been assured by the Abbot that they would emerge victorious if they carried the emblem into battle.

The combined Royalist forces planned to surprise the two Earls by intercepting them on their march to Cambridge at Fornham All Saints, near Bury, where they would have to ford the River Lark.

The two Earls, as they led their army across Suffolk towards Bury, received intelligence of the opposing forces arrayed against them, but they took no special precautions, confident that they outnumbered the Royalists by about four to one, and that they could easily defeat them in open battle.

But unbeknown to the rebels, the Royalist army had been swelled by a mass of peasants, armed with pitch-forks, flails and scythes, and that this huge force was laying in wait to attack them not in open battle, but as they forded the river. As the two Earls and their army began to cross the river, the Royalist knights charged, taking them by surprise and completely overwhelming them.

Realising that defeat was inevitable, High Bigod fled from the battle, escaping capture, and made his way to the safety of Framlingham Castle.

Countess Petronilla, seeing her husband surrounded and captured, also fled after throwing her rings and jewellery into the river, but fell head-first from the saddle into the muddy waters of a ditch when she urged her horse to cross it.

Royalist knights in pursuit of her, pulled her out to prevent her from drowning herself rather than face the ignominy of capture. She was taken back in shame to the victorious Richard de Lucy, who sent her to join her husband in captivity.

Meanwhile, the Flemish mercenaries, aware of the defeat, panicked and fled in all directions. They were pursued into the woods and marshes of the district by the incited peasants, who slaughtered them in great numbers with pitch-forks and scythes.

It is said that 10,000 rebels died that day, and that the River Lark ran red with their blood.

THE LAST OF HUGH BIGOD

The Earl and Countess of Leicester were transported to Normandy where they were imprisoned in the Royal Castle of Falaise. Hugh Bigod agreed to the offer of a truce during the winter on condition that he sent home all the remaining Flemish mercenaries.

He complied with the condition and the winter months passed peacefully, but in the Spring of 1174 widespread rebellions broke out again. The King of Scots invaded and captured most of Northern England, and the Count of Flanders, who was planning a full-scale invasion of the country, sent an expeditionary force which landed in the Orwell estuary in Suffolk.

Hugh soon raised his own forces and, swelled by the Flemish, set off to capture Norwich. They arrived at the city gates on 18th June and Bigod demanded the surrender of the city, but the people decided to stay loyal to the King.

Angered by their refusal, Bigod ordered his soldiers to break down the city gates with battering rams and scale the walls with ladders. The citizens were ill-prepared for such tactics; the walls were not manned, and the city itself was poorly defended. Nevertheless they furiously resisted the onslaught until the position became hopeless and they were forced to surrender.

Bigod then gave his soldiers permission to loot and burn the town after he had taken many of the principal citizens prisoner and held them to ransom.

Convinced that nothing could now prevent him from taking Norwich Castle, which was under the care of Sheriff Bartholomew de Glanville, who was residing at Orford Castle at the time. Bigod entered the fortress without a fight and immediately set about strengthening the castle's defences by deepening the ditches surrounding it.

King Henry, having dealt with the rebellion on the continent turned his attention to the troublesome Bigod, and marched into East Anglia with his army. He took Bigod's castles at Framlingham and Bungay with little resistance and gave instructions that they should both be demolished. He then advanced on Norwich.

The awesome sight of the surprise Royal forces mustered outside the walls of Norwich was enough to convince Bigod that resistance would be futile, and he sent word to the King that he was prepared to surrender.

The King took possession of Norwich Castle, and in the Great Hall, Bigod was forced to kneel before his sovereign, swear fealty and accept that his castles at Framlingham and Bungay were forfeited to the crown and were to be demolished. The King then demanded that Bigod pay a fine of 1000 marks, which Bigod gladly paid, thankful that he was fortunate to escape with his life after all the trouble he had caused.

Having lost his castles and authority Hugh Bigod considered it prudent to leave the Kingdom and embarked for the Continent where he joined the Count of Flanders on a pilgrimage to the Holy Land.

THE SICILIAN MISSION OF THE BISHOP OF NORWICH

The King of the Scots, who had occupied much of Northern England for some time, was eventually defeated by the East Anglian baron Ranulph de Glanville. He was taken captive and first held prisoner in Newcastle Castle, but was later moved to Falaise Castle in Normandy, where his fellow prisoners included the Earl and Countess of Leicester. Once all the rebels had been defeated, King Henry sent John of Oxford to Falaise to negotiate peace terms with the Scottish King. The terms that John demanded were harsh, but the Scottish King had little option but to agree to them.

He was forced to accept the conditions of the Treaty of Falaise, as it became known. This included him swearing fealty to the King of England as Overlord of Scotland, and handing over many of Scotland's greatest castles to English garrisons.

As a reward for bringing the Treaty to a satisfactory conclusion, John was created Bishop of Norwich, the position having fallen vacant following the death of William Turbe in January 1174.

Keen to take up the prestigious appointment, John was dismayed to find Norwich Cathedral in a sorry state when he arrived in the city for his enthronement.

A fire some years earlier had seriously damaged the Lady Chapel, but despite the efforts of the late Bishop Turbe, who had sat by the cathedral door, begging alms from worshippers for repair of the chapel, little work had been carried out and the Lady Chapel remained a disused ruin.

Following his enthronement Bishop John gave priority to restoring the Lady Chapel with enthusiasm, plus the building of an infirmary attached to the monastery.

But he had hardly settled down in his episcopate when the King ordered him to undertake what he described as a most important mission, and that Bishop John was the ideal man for the task. The King instructed him to journey to Palermo in the Kingdom of Sicily and oversee the marriage of his daughter, Princess Joan, to King William of Sicily.

After making hasty arrangements for the running of the cathedral during his absence, Bishop John set sail from Dover, despite ominous signs of bad weather ahead.

Shortly after the small ship left Dover, a gruesome storm broke. The wind blew with such fury causing enormous waves to toss the ship about mercilessly. Fortunately it managed to keep afloat, but all the crew and passengers were sick, bruised by being battered about and were thankful to reach the port of Barfluer in safety. The bishop and his entourage spent a few days in Barfluer to rest and recover from their ordeal.

As soon as he recovered, Bishop John set out overland on his long journey across France, first keeping to the provinces controlled by the King of England, but eventually had to cross hostile territory under the domination of French magnates.

He encountered little trouble, but was distressed to find the province of Auvergne suffering from a severe famine. The inhabitants could barely find sufficient fodder for their animals, let alone feed themselves. A chronicler recalls how the bishop was distressed by the sight and cries of so many hungry people, but he travelled on without ill-effects.

Arriving in the town of Valence, he looked forward to a few days rest, but the lodging house where he stayed afforded him little sleep as the beds were infested with fleas and bugs.

Plagued and bitten by the blood-sucking insects, he cut short his stay, and continued his journey over the Italian border to the Mediterranean Sea, where he boarded a boat that would take him to Sicily.

The boat, propelled by oarsmen, cruised down the Italian coast. But the sea was rough and the bishop suffered sea sickness for a second time, which added to the discomfort of the cramped, squalid conditions of his cabin on the boat.

He was relieved when the boat eventually landed on the Sicilian coast in August. But his relief was soon shattered when he realised that Sicily was suffering from an intense heatwave and a severe drought.

Nevertheless, after a few days rest, Bishop John continued his journey to the City of Palermo, where he was welcomed at the palace of King William. Soon after his arrival he took a major part in arranging the marriage ceremony of Princess Joanna to the Sicilian monarch.

The wedding, combined with the crowning of Joanna, took place on the 9th of November, 1176, at the Church of St. Giles. Shortly afterwards, Bishop John made preparations for his return journey to England.

Rather than face the long hazardous trek across land, he decided to endure the discomforts of returning by sea. Arriving safely in England he hastened on to Nottingham where the King was spending Christmas, and reported the successful completion of his mission. Bishop John then took leave of the King and returned to Norwich to take a well-earned rest in the comfort and luxury of his palace.

THE QUARRELSOME BIGODS

In 1177 news reached Norfolk that Earl Hugh Bigod had died in the Holy Land the previous year. The nature of his death is unrecorded, but it can be assumed that he died of natural causes as he was of a great age to have undertaken such a long journey to an inhospitable land.

The news of his death caused a bitter family dispute as to who was entitled to inherit his wealth and Earldom. Hugh had been married twice, firstly to Joanna de Vere, by whom he had a son named Roger, and secondly to Gundrada, who also bore him a son named Hugh after his father.

Roger, being the eldest son, naturally claimed the inheritance, but his stepmother, Gundrada, opposed his claim, stating that the family treasures and estates should rightfully pass to her son Hugh. A bitter feud broke out between Roger and Gundrada, stopping short of open hostilities.

As neither of them were prepared to compromise, Roger eventually appealed to the King to resolve the dispute, stressing his own claim to the Earldom.

The King, however, apparently tired of the troublesome Bigods, refused to endow the Earldom on either Roger or Hugh. Instead he confiscated all the Bigods' lands and made Roger answerable for all his late father's debts.

Although the King's decision shocked and surprised the Bigods, they dared not challenge it, and remained resentfully quiet for the remainder of King Henry's reign.

THE ELECTION OF ABBOT SAMSON

Abbot Hugh of Bury St. Edmunds had ruled the Abbey for 23 years, and in 1180 he decided to undertake a pilgrimage to Canterbury. Although a kind, gentle and devout man, he lacked the administrative skills that were necessary to organise the running of the abbey and its vast estates, and so his lax rule gradually led to the decay of buildings and the surrounding lands lying barren and waste.

To compensate for the loss of income from the abbey's estates, Abbot Hugh had borrowed large sums of money from the Jewish money-lenders of Norwich and Bury, often pawning the gold plate and precious ornaments of the church to meet the cost of running the abbey.

Seemingly unperturbed by the neglected state and mounting debts of the abbey, Hugh, old and losing his sight, set off for Canterbury on his personal mission, and all went well until he reached Rochester. Suddenly he fell from

The gateway of Waltham Abbey. – EARLY TWENTIETH CENTURY POSTCARD.

his horse and lay helpless on the ground, injured and unable to stand. His servants summoned medical aid and it was found that he had severely dislocated his kneecap.

After putting him through 'many discomforts', they decided they could do nothing for him on the spot, and directed that he should be conveyed back to his house at Bury on a horse drawn lifter. He was immediately confined to bed , but in spite of medical efforts, his knee injury festered and a fever set in.

Ironically, while the old Abbot lay dying, thieves broke into his house and stole everything, even the coverlet and blanket from his bed which covered him. He died on the 4th November 1180.

Bury Abbey continued to decline for two years after Abbot Hugh's death before King Henry gave permission for the election of a new abbot. During that period the monastery was ruled by the Prior.

The Prior naturally assumed that he would be elected, but after much wrangling over who should fill the vacant position, the monks could not agree on the most suitable candidate. Their indecisive bickering might have gone on for months if the King had not intervened, when all agreed that his choice of subsacrist, Samson of Tottington, was the ideal man for the job.

Samson was a Norfolk man of 'extreme sobriety' who had only been received into Holy Orders in 1166. He was duly given benediction by the Bishop of Winchester on the 28th February 1183 and soon proved himself worthy of election.

A skilled administrator with a shrewd perception of business matters, he quickly set about restoring the abbey's finances, stamping his authority over every aspect of the monastery. His fiery red beard presented a vivid indication of his temperament.

THE REFOUNDING OF WALTHAM ABBEY

After the murder of Thomas Beckett in 1170, King Henry, whose unwitting comment 'who will rid me of this turbulent priest' had instigated the crime, was filled with remorse, and swore to found three religious houses as a penance.

But his constant absences on the Continent, fighting to preserve the boundaries of his vast empire, not only left him little time to fulfil his pledge, but also deprived him of revenues to expend on the costly business of establishing monasteries.

As his vow weighed heavily upon his conscience, he decided that the cheapest alternative would be to refound already existing religious houses.

The first of those he chose to refound was Waltham Priory in Essex, where he turned out the secular canons without any means of support or maintenance, claiming they had neglected their duties and had lived immoral and debauched lives. He replaced them with Augustinians, appointing Ralph of Cirencester as Prior.

King Henry endowed his new foundation with the rich manor of Epping, bringing in enough money to improve their church. They immediately pulled down the east end of the building, installed a magnificent choir, several side chapels and a cloister.

In 1184, Waltham Priory was raised to the status of an abbey, exempt from the authority of the Bishop of London, being subject only to the King and the Pope.

The successive Abbot became a powerful figure, obtaining a seat in Parliament and, within a few years, Waltham Abbey became the wealthiest and most powerful religious house in Essex.

CHAPTER SIX

The Era of William Longchamp, 1185-1197

KING HENRY AT BURY

King Henry's turbulent life of being constantly on the move had taken its toll on him. When he arrived at Bury St. Edmunds in 1185 he looked weak and ill, and older than his 56 years. It was evident to Abbot Samson and the monks that Henry's days were numbered.

He had journeyed to Bury to pray at the shrine of St. Edmund, before once again crossing over to the Continent to settle a quarrel with his rebellious son, Richard, who had formed an alliance with the French king in an attempt to seize more of his father's lands.

Abbot Samson had long-harboured the notion of going on a pilgrimage to the Holy Land, and he took the opportunity during the King's stay to ask his permission to leave the abbey and journey to Jerusalem.

But the Bishop of Norwich, who was also present at the gathering, intervened, and persuaded the King not to allow Samson to leave the abbey as he himself had vowed to go on a crusade to the Holy Land, and it would endanger the security of the counties of Norfolk and Suffolk if he and the Abbot were absent at the same time. The King took the bishop's advice and refused Samson's request to leave the abbey and visit the Holy Land. Although he appeared disappointed by the refusal, Samson was probably relieved, as journeying to the Holy Land was a hazardous venture, but at least he had relieved his conscience by declaring his willingness to go.

He was even more relieved when the King departed from the abbey, as the cost of entertaining Royal guests and their accompanying entourage, was a considerable strain on the abbey's finances.

In his earlier days King Henry had led his armies triumphant on the Continent, but now that his health was failing fast, his soldiers deserted him and defected to Richard, his rebellious elder son, who, in spite of being given vast continental estates, was always ready to seize more.

Weak and ill, King Henry realised that he had no choice but to come to terms with his son, and agreed to recognise him as his heir. He also issued an amnesty to all who had conspired against him.

After giving in to his son, Henry was determined to travel back to his castle at Chinon to spend his last days. Whilst he lay dying, the castle was stripped of everything of value.

Even after his death on 6th July 1189. his corpse was stripped of royal finery, and his attendants had to cover his body with whatever garments they could find.

His body lay in State at Chinon for a few days before it was conveyed to Fortevrault, where it was buried in the Abbey church. Thus ended the turbulent reign of Henry II.

DISPOSAL OF THE BISHOPRIC OF ELY

Richard was now in control of all his father's domains by right of birth, but before setting off for England he visited Chinon as a matter of protocol to see his father's body where it lay in State at the castle.

It is said that he showed no emotion as he stood by his father's body, and that, when he took his leave, 'blood began to flow forthwith from the dead king's nostrils as if his spirit was moved with indignation'.

Richard was in no hurry to claim his kingdom. He had no rivals who dared to challenge his right to the throne and leisurely made his way across Normandy, and eventually landed at Portsmouth on 13th August 1189, where he was enthusiastically welcomed by the people, especially when he ordered the immediate release of all prisoners who had been imprisoned under his father's harsh laws.

He predictably acquired the name of Good King Richard, but the people were soon to experience another side of his character, for Richard had lived most of his life on the continent and had little to do with the English. He was first and foremost a soldier with grand ideas of leading a crusade to the Holy Land, and intended to use his new Kingdom's resources as a means of financing the venture.

One of his first acts when he reached Winchester on 15th August was to seize his father's personal wealth and secure the kingdom's treasury. To ensure that he remained in total control of the treasury, he appointed his loyal minion, William Longchamp, as Chancellor. Longchamp had served Richard faithfully as Chancellor of the Duchy of Aquitaine and was thoroughly familiar with his master's requirements.

The Bishop of Ely, Geoffrey Ridel, hastened to Winchester as soon as he heard that Richard had landed in England, as did many other bishops and nobles, to attend his coronation and pay homage to Richard as their new

King Richard was obsessed with leading a crusade, and intended using his Kingdom's resources to finance the venture.

King. But Geoffrey had not been in Winchester long when he was taken ill, and died within a few days. His body was conveyed to Ely where it was interred in the cathedral.

Although Richard no doubt outwardly expressed his sorrow at the untimely death of Bishop Ridel, he saw his death as a blessing, for the bishop had died intestate, and his personal fortune, consisting of 3000 gold marks, 2000 silver coins, plus gold and silver plate, jewels, rings, furniture and horses, was seized by Richard to swell much needed funds for his intended crusade to the Holy Land.

Richard was crowned King of England at Westminster Abbey on 15th September, 1189. Shortly afterwards he journeyed North to Pipewell Abbey, near Geddington. Northamptonshire, where he had summoned all the bishops and barons of England to attend a Great Council Meeting.

Having installed his most trusted servant, William Longchamp, as Chancellor, King Richard recognised the need for a skilful, trustworthy accountant to head the Treasury, and decided that Richard FitzNigel, Archdeacon of Ely, was the ideal man and should continue in the position he had held since 1169.

FitzNigel had long been a loyal servant to the crown, irrespective of whose head it rested upon. To ensure his continued loyalty King Richard also sanctioned his appointment as Bishop of London.

Obsessed with his determination to lead a crusade, King Richard took drastic actions to raise more money for the venture. Even the vast amount in his late father's treasury, or the unexpected windfall he seized from the intestate Bishop of Ely, was not sufficient to cover the massive cost of the enterprise.

To raise more money he first of all 'put up for sale all he had – officers, lordships, earldoms, castles, lands', then dismissed all the sheriffs and made them buy their Sheriffdoms back.

Even the vacant Bishopric of Ely was filled in a highly suspicious manner. The King had no authority to appoint a bishop, but he had the right to nominate one and order the chapter of the cathedral to elect his chosen nominee as bishop. He nominated William Longchamp, his Chancellor, to fill the vacant position, but his decision was no doubt influenced by Longchamp's payment of 4000 marks, which he claimed was in appreciation of his appointment as Chancellor.

THE SALE OF THE MANOR OF MILDENHALL
Constantly looking for ways of raising money, King Richard, decided to visit the rich abbey of Bury St. Edmunds on the 19th November, the day of the Feast of St. Edmund. His official purpose was to pay homage to St. Edmund, but his underlying motive was to raise money by offering to sell the Manor of Mildenhall to Abbot Samson.

Before the Norman Conquest, the Manor of Mildenhall had belonged to the Abbey of St. Edmund but had since been seized by the Crown. Abbot Samson, naturally, was keen to recover the Manor for the abbey, and offered the King 500 marks to purchase it outright.

King Richard, knowing the Manor would provide considerable profits for the abbey, refused the offer and said that nothing less than 1000 marks would secure the sale. Realising that the huge sum of 1000 marks would put a strain on the abbey's funds, but not wishing to get on the wrong side of the King, Samson reluctantly agreed to pay the higher price. After receiving the money, Richard immediately departed for London.

His fleet of 33 ships was being prepared in the Cinque Ports in readiness for the conveyance of his 9000 soldiers to the Holy Land, but before setting off he belatedly attempted to ensure that the government of England would be in safe hands during his absence.

Richard decided to appoint his loyal and trusted Chancellor, William Longchamp, Bishop of Ely, as Chief Justiciar and Regent of England south of the River Humber, and Bishop Hugh of Durham, as Chief Justiciar and Regent north of the River Humber. This hurried arrangement failed to define the powers of the joint Regents, but Longchamp's seniority appeared to have been confirmed when Richard gave him one of the Royal Seals and commanded him 'by means of it to have his orders carried out in the Kingdom', a command the power-hungry and ambitious Longchamp took seriously.

ROGER BIGOD BACK IN FAVOUR
Roger Bigod, son of the rebellious Hugh, secured favour with King Richard by contributing 1000 marks to his crusading funds, no doubt with the ultimate intention that such a generous gift would gain him rewards.

He was not disappointed. The King first made him a Steward of the Royal Household, and, convinced that he had proved his loyalty, restored the family estates to him.

Having gained the favour of the King, Roger Bigod lost no time in planning the rebuilding of his castle at Framlingham. He ordered that the castle should be a massive fortress of masonry, befitting his status and reminding people of the power of the Bigods.

Even more status came Roger's way when King Richard created him Earl of Norfolk and gave him the Constableship of Norwich Castle before sailing for the continent on 11th December 1189.

Thus the Bigods' were now fully restored to their position of power and authority in East Anglia.

The King had spent little more than four months in his Kingdom before setting off to the Holy Land, during which time, as one chronicler put it, he was 'permanently on the prowl, always searching for the weak spot where there is something for him to steal', and, because of his restless nature, many of his subjects thought that he would never return to England.

THE ENTHRONEMENT OF WILLIAM LONGCHAMP

When the Bishopric of Ely was created in 1109 the abbey was reduced to the status of a Priory, which meant that its church not only served the Priory, but also contained the throne, or cathedra, of the bishop of the newly-created diocese.

William Longchamp, who had been consecrated at Lambeth on 31st December 1189, travelled to Ely in the New Year for his enthronement as the fourth Bishop of Ely. Prior Richard and brethren of the Priory might well have been apprehensive of his arrival, for Longchamp was the most powerful man in England, and had a reputation of being ruthless, ambitious and utterly unscrupulous.

When he eventually arrived in Ely, the sight of him must have come as a shock to the monks and dignitaries assembled at the Priory, for far from being the upright dignitary they expected, William Longchamp was a short, dwarfish man with crooked legs, which made him walk like a cripple. According to one chronicler 'his neck was short, his back was humped, his belly stuck out in front and his buttocks at the back'.

The same chronicler likened him to an ape, describing his head as big with hair on his forehead coming down almost to his eyebrows. His complexion was dark with little sunken eyes, a flat nose, a shaggy beard, receding chin and an almost continuous grin.

The grandson of a Norman serf, he was as ugly on the inside as he was on the outside, foul and offensive to the English, for whom he had nothing but

The magnificent Norman nave of Ely Cathedral, the setting for Longchamp's enthronement as bishop. – COURTESY OF THE CAMBRIDGESHIRE COLLECTION.

hatred and contempt. Refusing to utter a word in English, he spoke only Norman French.

No doubt Prior Richard was greatly relieved when the new bishop departed for London shortly after his enthronement, as Longchamp expected only the most lavish accommodation for himself and his large retinue of servants, attendants and soldiers. A lengthy stay in Ely could well have bankrupted the Priory.

REGENT OF ENGLAND

When he returned to London, Bishop Longchamp took up residence in the Tower, the custody of which he had been given by King Richard prior to his departure for the Holy Land.

Longchamp began to strengthen the defences of the mighty fortress by building a wall on the north-west side and digging a deep ditch around the castle. He also brought an army of mercenaries from the Continent for his own personal protection.

Having fortified the castle and increased the number of his personal armed guards, Longchamp was confident that his position as co-regent of England in the absence of the King was secure enough to rule the whole Kingdom in accordance with the monarch's vague orders.

Obsessed by power, Longchamp began by undermining that of his fellow

125

As Regent of England, Bishop Longchamp took up residence in the Tower of London.

co-regent, Bishop Hugh of Durham, by barring him from attending meetings of the Exchequer. Not surprisingly Longchamp's display of arrogance led to a fierce quarrel between the co-regents, for Bishop Hugh was a proud and immensely rich prelate who looked down on the low-born Longchamp as an untrustworthy upstart.

To settle the dispute, Longchamp invited Bishop Hugh to meet him at Tickhill, Nottinghamshire, where he produced a document bearing the King's seal, which gave him absolute authority over all England.

As the Royal Seal was in Longchamp's possession, Hugh voiced his suspicions that the document had been forged. Enraged by this assumption, Longchamp had Bishop Hugh seized and taken to London, where he was held prisoner in the Tower.

Bishop Hugh was only released after accepting that the document was genuine, agreeing to keep the King's peace and surrendering his castles at Newcastle and Windsor to Longchamp.

Having peacefully crushed his closest rival, Bishop William Longchamp was now Regent of all England.

TERRORISM AND EXTORTION
After humiliating and defeating the Bishop of Durham, William Longchamp had control of many of the greatest fortifications in England and complete

power over the Kingdom, with the exception of the West Country where Prince John, the King's brother held sway.

Longchamp treated all the nobles and clergy in the rest of the country with arrogance and indifference but dare not challenge the authority and power of Prince John.

In June 1190 Pope Clement, at the request of King Richard, appointed Longchamp Papal Legate of all England, Wales and parts of Ireland. This gave him supreme power and authority over the Church. Even Archbishops now had to succumb to his will, and he became more aloof and arrogant than ever.

Full of pride, Longchamp toured the realm in stately style, accompanied by a vast retinue of attendants and an army of 1000 soldiers.

'His pomp,' wrote one chronicler, 'in almost everything, exceeded that of a King'. Indeed, on his triumphant travels throughout the land, he extracted money from every rank of person, not only to satisfy the King's constant demands for money to sustain the crusade, but also to support his own extravagant lifestyle.

The county sheriffs were given a free rein to gather in taxes by whatever means they could, so generally they resorted to intimidation by surrounding themselves with soldiers 'by whose lawless and unrestrained violence, innumerable outrages and enormities were committed in the different counties'.

The people suffered badly from Longchamp's tyranny; the monasteries were brought to the verge of ruin by his rapacity, the clergy oppressed by the power he exerted over them, and the nobility were disgusted by his pride and insolence.

Longchamp terrorised the whole Kingdom to such an extent that a chronicler wrote, 'no-one in the realm dare resist him. either in word or deed'.

RUMBLINGS OF DISCONTENT

Obsessed by his own power and unopposed rule, Bishop Longchamp felt completely secure in his position of overall authority. He ignored the peoples' feeble complaints, and even brought a troupe of French minstrels from the continent to tour English towns and sing his praises.

They were especially ordered to sing his favourite couplet, which he considered most suitable.

The lyrics ran as follows:

'You do such great things so easily and so well.
That whether you are god or man one cannot tell'.

A troupe of French minstrels was sent around England to sing the praises of Bishop Longchamp.

The minstrel troupe received a lukewarm reception on their tour, for no amount of singing the praises of Longchamp could reverse the deep mistrust the people had for him, and rumblings of discontent were common at all public gatherings.

The abbots and bishops resented the authority Longchamp had over them, as did the barons. They all considered him to be a jumped up peasant whose dictatorial rule over the land had to be curtailed, and looked for a leader to resist the tyrant. They found such a man in Prince John the King's brother, who had quietly arrived in England in 1191.

Prince John considered himself heir to the throne and agreed to oppose Longchamp. The discontented barons and clergy rallied to him. The barons began to strengthen their castles and fortify their towns, more as a show of solidarity against Longchamp's rule than preparations for an all-out war against him, for hardly anyone desired to start what would inevitably be a bloody conflict.

Prince John was the only man Longchamp feared, he was aware that in the event of King Richard's death on crusade that John would become King, which meant he would loose overall power and authority.

When he heard that the clergy and barons were conspiring against him, the thought that Prince John might become King began to haunt Longchamp, until the idea came to him that if, with the backing of the King of Scots, Arthur of Brittany, the 3-year-old nephew of King Richard, was named as the rightful heir to the throne, he could hold power over the boy and continue to act as Regent.

When news leaked to Prince John of Longchamp's intention, he mustered his supporters and seized the castles of Nottingham and Tickhill, which had been under the control of the Regent.

Longchamp, at last realising the extent of opposition against him and not wishing to plunge the kingdom into civil war, agreed to try and settle differences with Prince John by arbitration. They met at Winchester, but both parties were prepared for war if all else failed.

Longchamp arrived at Winchester, supported by William de Albini, Earl of Arundel, Richard de Clare, and Hamelin de Warenne, Earl of Surrey, as well as 2000 knights and a large number of Welsh soldiers, but, in spite of this show of military strength, Longchamp was strongly advised and persuaded to sign a treaty with Prince John agreeing 'not to see the Prince's disinheritance but would do everything in his power to advance him to the throne' if the King should die on crusade.

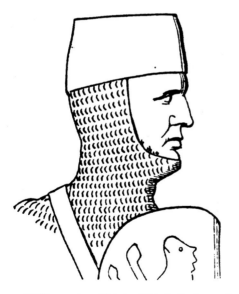

William de Albini, Chief Butler of England, Lord of Rising and Buckenham, Earl of Arundel and supporter of Bishop Longchamp.

Prince John had become increasingly aware of Longchamp's power and was somewhat relieved to see him sign the treaty. But the devious bishop was not accustomed to humiliating defeat and fled to the Tower of London, which he had previously stocked with a plentiful supply of provisions and arms.

THE FALL OF LONGCHAMP

Bishop Longchamp was constantly seeking ways to increase his power and wealth by any means. Since the death of the Archbishop of York in 1181, the See had remained vacant, and he had ambitions of being elected to the Archbishopric.

But his ambitions were thwarted when King Richard appointed his half-brother, Geoffrey Plantagenet, to the vacant office. Geoffrey arrived in England in September

1191 to take up his appointment, but on landing at Dover news reached him that Longchamp had ordered the Constable of Dover Castle to arrest him.

Geoffrey thereupon sought sanctuary in St. Martin's Priory Church, but in vain, for Longchamp had little respect for the Church, or the sanctuary it provided. He ordered his men to enter the church, by force if necessary.

They broke down the door and found Geoffrey in prayer before the altar. They seized him, hauled him out of the church, then dragged him through the streets by the legs and threw him into the dungeon at Dover Castle.

This brutal act outraged every clergyman in the country, and the angry bishops promptly called for a meeting, which was held in the graveyard of St. Paul's Church. The bishops unanimously agreed that Bishop Longchamp had over-reached himself by abusing his authority, and should be excommunicated.

Prince John seized the opportunity to organise his supporters, and they marched through the streets of London to the Tower intent on capturing Longchamp. But Longchamp, desperate to escape capture by his enemies, had fled to Dover. There he changed his priests' robes and donned a woman's green gown.

Satisfied that no-one would recognise him disguised as a woman, he ventured to the harbour and waited while his servants searched for a vessel that would carry him across the Channel.

But as he stood on the quayside dressed as a woman, impatiently waiting, the last thing he expected was to be mistaken for a harlot. An amorous fisherman approached him in a unmistakable manner assuming that the 'harlot' would mutually respond to his advances.

A chronicler remarked that the fisherman 'put his left arm around the bishop's neck while his right hand roamed lower down.

The bishop stood in stunned amazement while the fisherman pulled up his gown and was 'confronted with the irrefutable evidence that the woman was a man'. The fisherman called his mates to have a look at this 'remarkable creature'.

Their taunts and derisive remarks at the distraught Longchamp soon attracted a mob who began throwing stones at the once-mighty bishop. Eventually they seized him, spat on him, and dragged him through the streets of Dover to an inn where they locked him in a cellar.

Longchamp languished in the cellar for a week until Prince John heard of his sorry plight and intervened. The Prince firstly deposed the bishop of all his secular offices, then mercifully ordered his release.

After his experience as a prisoner in the cellar, the humiliated Longchamp thought it wise to depart from England, and shortly after his release set sail for Flanders.

EXCOMMUNICATION OF LONGCHAMP

Although humiliated and disgraced, Longchamp would not accept his deposition from secular office by Prince John. He reasoned that as King Richard had appointed him Regent and Chancellor, only the King was entitled to remove him from the positions.

He wrote a letter to Pope Celestine III complaining of the treatment he had undergone at the instigation of the English clergy. The Pope sympathised with Longchamp and wrote an open letter to the bishops of England urging them to excommunicate Prince John and his advisors.

But the Pope's letter was ignored, mainly by the insistence of Prince John's chief advisor, Archbishop Walter of Coustance, who had assumed the role of Chief Justiciar and Chancellor.

Archbishop Walter, the arch-enemy of Longchamp, excommunicated the exiled bishop, and sequestrated the revenues of the diocese of Ely.

Hearing the news, Longchamp retaliated by excommunicating Archbishop Walter and, in addition, put the diocese of Ely under an interdict, which meant that no mass, or any service, could be celebrated, no-one could marry, and the dead had to be buried in unconsecrated ground.

This unhappy situation continued for some time, until Queen Eleanor the King's mother, decided to visit her manors in the diocese of Ely. Upon arrival she was petitioned by the inhabitants of the villages, who requested her to intervene in the bitter quarrel between the rival parties.

Queen Eleanor took notice of the villagers' complaints, and ordered Archbishop Walter to lift the excommunication on Longchamp and return the revenues of his bishopric to him. In return, Longchamp had little choice but to lift the excommunication on Archbishop Walter and the interdict on his diocese.

Having gained favour with Queen Eleanor, Longchamp decided to set sail for England and regain all his former positions. Styling himself Legate of the Apostolic See and Lord Chancellor of England he landed at Dover and stayed with his sister, Richeut, the wife of Matthew de Clare, Constable of Dover Castle

But the barons and bishops were still hostile towards him and were not prepared to accept his return to power. Fearing trouble, Queen Eleanor sent him a message urging him to leave England. Longchamp took her advice and once again returned to Normandy.

THE RANSOM

King Richard was kept informed of the unstable political situation in England and was strongly advised to return to his kingdom and sort out the problems.

In 1193 he took ship from the Holy land, anticipating a quick solution to the political problems back home, and a speedy return to the crusade. But his ship ran into a violent storm in the Adriatic Sea and was wrecked. Fortunately the ship was close to shore, and King Richard and his retainers with most of the crew, somehow managed to reach the shore safely.

After recovering from their ordeal, King Richard and his retinue were forced to continue their journey overland, through the territory of Duke Leopold of Austria who was, at the time, hostile to Richard after a disagreement between them when they were on crusade together.

Hoping to avoid recognition, Richard dressed as a pilgrim to undertake the journey, but was soon recognised by some Austrian soldiers. He was immediately arrested and imprisoned in the grim castle of Durnstein, a stronghold situated high on a rocky crag overlooking the River Danube.

Bishop Longchamp, exiled in Normandy, was one of the first to hear of the King's capture. He sent out his spies, who discovered that Duke Leopold had handed Richard over to the Emperor of Germany, and was held captive in the castle of Trifels, high in the mountains of Bavaria.

Longchamp hurried to see his master at Trifels and offered whatever assistance he could to free him from captivity, but was shocked to hear that the Emperor was demanding a ransom of 100,000 marks before he would release him.

The enormous sum would be difficult to raise, Richard having drained his kingdom of revenue to finance his participation in the crusade. Nevertheless, Richard instructed Longchamp to return to England and raise the ransom money by whatever means possible.

Richard sent letters to his mother, Queen Eleanor, and the barons and bishops of England urging them to allow his 'dearest chancellor' to organise the collecting of the ransom money. But before they would allow Longchamp into the country they made him swear an oath not to meddle in the affairs of state.

Longchamp reluctantly agreed to their demand, and declared that he returned as 'a simple bishop'. He landed at Ipswich, and after spending the night at Hitcham went on to Bury St. Edmunds where he intended to hear mass. Abbot Samson, believing that Longchamp was still under excommunication and that any form of divine celebration was prohibited in his presence, immediately stopped the service when he saw Longchamp enter the church.

At first Longchamp pretended not to notice, but when the service did not recommence he flew into a rage and a bitter argument ensued between him and Abbot Samson. As the fracas continued, Samson received word that the excommunication on Longchamp had been lifted, and the two prelates came to terms and exchanged a 'kiss of peace'.

COLLECTING THE RANSOM

The huge sum demanded by the Emperor of Germany for the release of King Richard caused many arguments between the authorities in England as to how it could best be raised.

But Longchamp, an old hand at extorting money, suggested to the Queen Mother ways of raising the ransom. The barons and particularly Archbishop Walter were still distrustful of Longchamp, whereupon the Queen Mother thought it prudent to send Longchamp back to Germany and inform the King of the plans made to collect the ransom.

She issued orders to all Justiciars and Sheriffs to impose a levy of 25% tax on all income, with the exception of the parish clergy who were allowed to pay a tenth of their income, with the promise that every parish church, as well as the monasteries, must surrender all gold and silver plate. In addition the Cistercian and Gilbertine monasteries were to give their wool crop for a year.

When the money was collected it was to he sent to St. Paul's Cathedral in the care of Richard FitzNigel, Bishop of London and State Treasurer, who was to account for it in a separate exchequer.

But, unlike a fixed-tax amount, no-one was certain what collective sum could be collected from each individual or how much plate every parish church contained, so Richard FitzNigel had no idea what to expect from each shire.

The hastily formed system was open to abuse by dishonest sheriffs who found it easy to line their own pockets, none more so than Osbert de Longchamp, Sheriff of Norfolk and Suffolk, and the brother of the Bishop of Ely.

Collecting the ransom money was like a gift from heaven to the rapacious Osbert, who appears to have been even more obnoxious that his brother. Corrupt and greedy, he was in his element bullying the people to part with a fourth of their earnings, and threatening the clergy to part with whatever he considered to be a tenth of their income.

Even the Gilbertine Canons were

A Gilbertine Monk.

given no quarter. Although they belonged to the only purely English monastic order in the country, owning just one priory in East Anglia at Shouldham in Norfolk, which had been established in 1193.

The Priory was endowed with lands in 26 Norfolk parishes where it pastured sheep, wool being its chief source of income, so it was a bitter blow to the Canons when they were ordered to give up the wool crop for a year to help ransom an absent monarch. But Sheriff Osbert showed no compassion when he seized the crop and left them to struggle in poverty for a year.

It was a different story when the collectors arrived at the wealthy abbey of Bury St. Edmunds. Abbot Samson adamantly refused to allow them to strip the gold leaf from the shrine of St. Edmund, saying that if they did, the Saint would avenge such sacrilege.

Fearing the curse of St. Edmund and also the wrath of the powerful and influential Abbot, the collectors left the shrine untouched in its golden splendour.

At the end of the year the accumulated sum collected and deposited in St. Paul's fell far short of the ransom demanded, no doubt due to the collectors purloining a proportion for themselves, and Richard FitzNigel had little choice but to send them out again to gather more money.

Eventually enough was collected to satisfy the German Emperor and the gold and silver coins were shipped to the continent in expectation of the King's immediate release.

THE RESTORATION OF WILLIAM LONGCHAMP

Prince John, who had allied himself to the King of France with the intention of seizing and sharing all Richard's lands on the Continent between them, offered the German Emperor 30,000 marks if he would delay the release of Richard.

When the bishops and barons heard of this treacherous act they declared that John should forfeit all his lands and castles in England as a punishment. After lengthy negotiations between the Queen Mother, Longchamp and the German Emperor, King Richard was released on the 4th February 1194, and returned safely to England, landing at Sandwich harbour on the 13th March.

Following short stays at Canterbury and London, he went to Bury St. Edmunds, accompanied by Longchamp, whom he had reinstated as his Chancellor, there they were lavishly entertained by Abbot Samson.

But the King was anxious to set off for Nottingham, where he intended to re-take the castle which was still held by supporters of Prince John, so, after paying his respects to St. Edmund and thanking Abbot Samson for his hospitality, he left Bury with his entourage for Nottingham the following day.

He took the castle with little difficulty, but the success failed to console

him. His failure to capture the Holy City from the Saracens and his long imprisonment in Germany still haunted him. He became bitter towards the English, and openly accused them of being mean and slow in paying the ransom to secure his release.

After taking Nottingham Castle, Richard summoned a meeting of the Great Council. He now wanted more money in order to raise an army to repel the King of France who had invaded Normandy, and was determined to squeeze every penny he could from his subjects.

Although Richard had reinstated William Longchamp as Chancellor, the important but unenviable task of finding and collecting more money was given to Archbishop Hubert of Canterbury. Richard felt confident that he would succeed.

The King was anxious to return to the continent and left Nottingham, reaching St. Swithin's Priory, Winchester on 15th April. During his stay there, he decided to stage a second coronation as a demonstration to all the bishops and barons assembled for the event that he was their King and overlord.

The ceremony duly took place and was conducted by the Archbishop of Canterbury. William Longchamp and Richard FitzNigel had the honoured position of standing either side of the King.

After his impressive second Coronation King Richard journeyed to Portsmouth where he took a ship to the continent, accompanied by his faithful Chancellor. Neither of them were destined to return.

THE DEATH OF WILLIAM LONGCHAMP

Although he continued to hold the office of Chancellor, Longchamp held no secular authority in England, but remained in Normandy faithfully serving his King.

He undertook several diplomatic missions, including arranging a truce with the King of France, and then secretly visited the German Emperor to ask his assistance to invade France. A double deal that appealed to the deceitful and wily old bishop.

In January 1197 he was sent on a mission to Rome but was taken seriously ill after reaching Poitier. In spite of efforts to cure him, he died there on the 30th January.

It is said that at the very moment he expired, tears flowed from a crucifix in Poitier Cathedral, but in England, according to a chronicler, 'The people rejoiced at his death'.

Longchamp's body was buried in the Abbey of Le Pin after his heart was removed and brought to Ely where it was buried in the cathedral.

CHAPTER SEVEN

Rebellion of the Barons, 1198-1217

TWO CEREMONIES AT WESTMINSTER

It was almost six months after the death of William Longchamp before the monks of Ely elected Eustachius, Dean of Salisbury, to become the new Bishop of Ely.

No doubt their choice was influenced by the King, as Eustachius had been Vice-chancellor to Longchamp and, after being elected as bishop, he was also promoted to fill the vacant office of Chancellor.

In early 1198 he was sent to Germany on his first diplomatic mission to ensure that Otto, King Richard's nephew, would be the next Holy Roman Emperor. The mission was successful, and shortly after his return to England he was consecrated Bishop of Ely by the Archbishop of Canterbury in St. Catherine's Chapel, Westminster Abbey.

In the Spring of 1199 whilst besieging the castle at Chalus, the King was struck in the shoulder by a bolt fired from a crossbow. The bolt penetrated well into the flesh and the operating surgeon had to cut deep to remove it. The wound was so bad that gangrene quickly set in and, after twelve painful days of suffering, King Richard died.

According to his wishes, Richard's body, clothed in his coronation robes, was

Prince John succeeded his brother as king, and was crowned in Westminster Abbey.

buried in a tomb close to his father's in Fontevrault Abbey, his brain and intestines were buried near the spot where he died, and his heart buried in Rouen in a silver casket.

Prince John was in Brittany when he received the news of his brother's death and hastened to Rouen, where he was immediately acknowledged as Duke of Normandy. He never expected to ascend to the throne of England and inherit so much power, and far from grieving over his brother's death, he could hardly contain his true feelings.

John, the youngest of King Henry's children, was a cunning, slothful, plump little man who was ill-suited for the role of monarch. Nevertheless, he eagerly crossed the Channel and entered London on 24th May 1199.

Shortly afterwards he was crowned King of England in Westminster Abbey.

THE KING'S HENCHMAN

Like the majority of his predecessors John soon realised that he was handicapped to carry out his role as monarch due to a shortage of money.

There was insufficient revenue to enable him to raise a force to repel the French King, who was again encroaching on the Angevin possessions on the Continent, and John desperately needed more money to oppose the French King. He found the ideal tax collector in Geoffrey FitzPeter, who had risen from a lowly knight to become one of the premier barons in the land after marrying Lady Beatrice, a descendent of the Mandervilles, who claimed the Earldom of Essex.

FitzPeter had opposed the tyrannical rule of Bishop Longchamp and had succeeded him as Chief Justiciar of England following the bishop's death. He assumed the title, Earl of Essex, supported Prince John, and played a major role in securing the prince's succession to the throne.

He was well rewarded for his loyalty after the King's coronation, not only being given large grants of land, but also being officially invested with the Earldom of Essex and confirmed as Chief Justiciar.

Although John is said to have disliked FitzPeter, he accepted that he was well suited to act as his chief henchman and had no doubt that in his role as Chief Justiciar he could trust him to act as Regent whenever he was away on the Continent.

FitzPeter made his base at the Tower of London. A well-educated man, he was fluent in Latin and had a good understanding of law and mathematics, but was harsh in temperament and had no hesitation in imposing extortionate taxes on the people.

He served his master faithfully by giving the sheriffs a free hand to collect taxes by whatever means they chose. He also issued orders that they should impose the laws of the forest and severely punish any person who encroached, or poached in the Royal Forests.

Not surprisingly, FitzPeter, and the majority of the sheriffs, soon became very unpopular. The people even voiced that of all the King's 'evil counselors', FitzPeter was the worst.

Although he upset the people by imposing harsh taxes and laws, he encouraged many towns to seek self-government, and issued Charters and privileges to them. Several major towns in East Anglia benefited from this. Ipswich, for instance was granted special privileges by being exempted from the payment of lastage, a tax levied on all market traders entering the town, and also stallage, a tax imposed on all stalls in the market.

This undoubtedly helped to boost trade in Ipswich market and improve its popularity. FitzPeter also made Yarmouth a free burgh, granted special privileges to Cambridge, King's Lynn and Norwich, from which they all benefited.

But, like many noblemen of the time, he was concerned about the well-being of his soul, and that, when his time came to depart from this earthly life, his repented sins would be forgiven and he would enter heaven.

To ensure he stayed on the right side of God, he patronised the abbey of Walden, and also founded a priory at Shouldham, in Norfolk, for Gilbertine Canons and Nuns, and endowed it with several manors and six churches.

THE AFFLUENT TOWN

The charters and privileges to Norwich by Geoffrey FitzPeter were the latest in a series obtained by the burgesses since the building of the castle, which not only raised the status of the town but also increased its size and importance as a trading centre.

Instead of paying frequent taxes, tolls and rents to the King, the charter allowed the populace to pay a fixed lump sum annually, giving more power to the burgesses and relieving the Sheriff of many of the town's mundane affairs.

The granting of the charters consequently led to the increase of wealth in Norwich, mainly due to foreign trade. Ships from Cologne, Flanders, Sweden, Italy and elsewhere, could sail up the River Wensum and discharge their merchandise at the town's quays.

Stallholders and shopkeepers grew rich on imported goods, such as wine, furs, woollen cloth, silk, beeswax, sugar, spices and steel. This affluence afforded a steady flow of immigrants from the countryside.

As the population grew, the town walls and defences had to be extended, and the increase in wealth allowed the building of the cathedral to progress at a steady pace and, by the early 13th century, 47 parish churches within the town were under various stages of construction.

The extensive building work led to increased activity in the town. A steady flow of masonry, imported from Caen, and vast quantities of oak from English forests drew a considerable number of labourers to the town from far and wide, including highly-skilled craftsmen, such as masons, wood carvers and workers in glass and metal, who set up their own communities.

It is estimated that 37,000 tons of stone were used in building the town walls alone, and that probably a similar quantity was used in the building of Norwich Cathedral and churches.

During the increased bustle in the town, the Bishop, John of Oxford, decided to retire from political life and retreated to the luxury of his palace. Old and worn out by a life of service to the monarch, he devoted the rest of his time to charity and the patronage of writers.

A highly respected and beloved ecclesiastic, he passed away on the 2nd January 1200, a day all building work presumably stopped and did not resume until he had been laid to rest in the cathedral.

One of the late bishop's last duties had been to attend King John's coronation, and when the King heard of the cleric's death, he allowed the bishopric to remain vacant for a few months, not as a gesture of respect, but so that the vast income from the bishopric went directly into his own coffers.

Having swelled his treasury, King John, who was always in need of money, allowed the vacancy to be filled in September 1200, but ensured that his nominee, John de Grey, Archdeacon of Gloucester, was chosen for the position.

John de Grey was said to be a native of Norfolk who had long been in the service of the King. He had served the King faithfully, but old chroniclers regarded him as one of the 'evil counselors, a slimy toady who was entirely beloved by the King'.

At his consecration as Bishop of Norwich on 24th September 1200, no-one could have foreseen the turmoil that John de Grey and King John would eventually cause in the Kingdom.

THE LAKENHEATH MARKET DISPUTE

In 1201, Eustace, Abbot of Flay , came from France to visit the Abbey of Bury St. Edmunds. He preached in the market place, where he called upon the men of the town to join a crusade against the Saracens. He also spoke out to the market traders against public buying and selling on the Sabbath.

Later, in the privacy of Abbot Samson's palace, Eustace admonished Samson for allowing such a sinful practice as Sunday trading and advised him to transfer the market day to a Tuesday. But when the Abbot of Flay had left, Samson, who was not one who took kindly to being told what to do, transferred the market to a Wednesday.

Not long after the Abbot of Flay's visit, the monks of Ely, under the orders of their Prior, set up a Wednesday market at Lakenheath, which soon began to take trade away from the market at Bury.

As Lakenheath fell within the Liberty of St. Edmund, Abbot Samson wrote to Prior Hugh of Ely asking him to stop the enterprise, but the stubborn prior claimed they had permission to hold the market by Royal Charter. Samson then complained to King John that the market at Lakenheath was injurious to the long-established one at Bury.

King John replied to the effect that he had granted the Prior of Ely permission to hold a weekly market on the condition that it would not be in competition with, or 'damage' neighbouring markets, and then on payment of 40 marks, issued Abbot Samson with a charter that effectively forbade any market to be held within the Liberty of St. Edmund without the Abbot's permission.

Having obtained the charter from the King, Samson was determined to stop Prior Hugh's enterprise at Lakenheath, he approached the Chief Justiciar, Geoffrey FitzPeter, and asked him to intervene and order Prior Hugh to close the market at Lakenheath.

Not wanting to get involved, FitzPeter passed the matter on to the Sheriff of Suffolk and ordered him to deal with it. But the Sheriff had no jurisdiction in the Liberty of St. Edmund and wrote to Abbot Samson telling him that he must enforce his own charter.

Samson then ordered his bailiff to gather together a force of armed horsemen and 'destroy the market' at Lakenheath. Accompanied by 600 horsemen, the bailiff entered Lakenheath at night but found the market deserted, the stall-holders having fled after being forewarned.

Expecting trouble, the Prior of Ely, with an equally powerful armed force, was in residence in his manor house, but to avoid bloodshed decided not to interfere, while the Bury men destroyed the market stalls, and drove all the animals in the cattle market away.

Although Prior Hugh made strenuous efforts to recover the stolen cattle, chroniclers of the time do not record the outcome, but it seems obvious that Abbot Samson's forceful action led to the closure of the Lakenheath market after its short existence.

CONFLICT WITH THE POPE

Hubert Walter, Archbishop of Canterbury, had been Chancellor of England for several years and had proved to be an efficient administrator, although at times he could be over-scrupulous and had often frustrated King John's plans.

When John heard the news of Hubert Walter's death in July 1205, he appeared to be relieved by exclaiming, 'Now, I am King!'

With the old, interfering Chancellor out of the way he could now fill two vacant posts with minions who would do his bidding. He chose Walter de Grey to fill the post of Chancellor, and nominated his faithful servant John de Grey, Bishop of Norwich, as the new Archbishop of Canterbury.

But the monks of Canterbury, who were not even consulted, immediately objected, having traditionally a say in the election of an Archbishop, refused to accept the King's choice.

They subsequently elected their Sub-Prior, Reginald, as their choice for Archbishop and secretly sent messengers to Rome to obtain the Pope's approval of their election.

When news of this 'secret mission' leaked to King John he flew into a rage and promptly sent emissaries to Rome to obtain the Pope's confirmation of John de Grey as Archbishop.

But King John had not reckoned on the forceful character who occupied the Papal Throne. Pope Innocent III, as Christ's Vicar on Earth, considered himself to be 'below God but above kings and emperors' and was not prepared to bend to the demands of mere kings.

Pope Innocent III considered himself above kings, and imposed an interdict on England.

Pope Innocent refused to accept either John de Grey or Reginald as Archbishop, and considered that the best interests of the Church in England would be served by the appointment of Cardinal Stephen Langton.

Langton, a renowned scholar and theologian who had lived and studied in Paris most of his life, was consecrated Archbishop of Canterbury on 17th June 1206, by the Pope at Viterbo, Italy.

King John was furious with the Pope and would not accept Langton as the new Archbishop. He refused to allow him to set foot in England, and blamed the monks of Canterbury for causing the dispute.

THE INTERDICT

Eustachius, Bishop of Ely, had long been highly regarded for his wisdom, and had frequently been employed by Pope Innocent III to fulfil delicate ecclesiastical missions. The Pope believed that if anyone could persuade King John to accept Langton as Archbishop, then Eustachius was the man.

If John was not influenced by the persuasive talents of Eustachius, then he was to be threatened with an interdict on the entire kingdom. But King John stubbornly refused to accept Langton, in spite of the persistent efforts of Eustachius.

On hearing of the bishop's failure Pope Innocent ordered him to pronounce the interdict, which he did, and then made a hasty exit to France to escape the King's wrath.

Following the pronouncement of the Interdict, the doors of churches and cathedrals were closed and locked, no service or Mass could be performed and no sacraments given to the dying. The dead could not he buried in consecrated ground, but had to be buried in fields or by the roadside, marriages could not be solemnised, but baptisms were allowed to take place in the church porch.

The monks of the Cistercian order claimed exemption from the Interdict and continued to hold services in their monasteries. Whilst the bells of Norfolk churches remained silent those of the Cistercian Priory at Shouldham rang out in defiance. They were severely rebuked by the Pope.

Later in the year, the Pope ordered Eustachius to try again to agree terms with King John. The bishop was given safe conduct to cross the Channel, and met King John at Chilham Castle, in Kent, but all his efforts were in vain. The stubborn monarch would not change his mind, and, disillusioned, Eustachius returned to France.

Immediately after Eustachius arrived back in France, the Pope instructed him to prepare and issue an excommunication on King John, and have it published throughout the kingdom. Wearied by his frustrated efforts, Eustachius refused to cross the Channel again, and issued the excommunication from the safety of French soil.

But the bishops of England feared the King and, according to one chronicler, reacted 'like dumb dogs', not daring to publish the excommunication, but fled the country in fear of King John's retribution.

THE FIGHTING BISHOP

Unlike his fellow bishops, John de Grey, Bishop of Norwich, remained loyal to his royal master, ever hopeful that he would emerge from the dispute as Archbishop of Canterbury.

King John, however, had other plans for his faithful bishop.

Ireland, which King John claimed as part of his kingdom, was a lawless land ruled by minor kings and chieftains, vying for power with the Norman barons who had acquired large land holdings along the east coast.

Two Norman barons were a particular nuisance. William de Braose, Lord of Limerick, and Hugh de Lacy, Lord of Ulster, arrogantly defied the King's authority and acted as independent princes.

John de Grey was appointed Viceroy of Ireland, with specific instructions to introduce English laws, and subdue the Irish kings into feudal barons holding their lands directly from the English crown.

Taking up residence in Dublin Castle, the Bishop of Norwich soon discovered there was little he could do without the backing of a large army.

In 1210 King John landed near Waterford with a large army. Joined by the Bishop of Norwich, he pursued the rebellious barons to Carrickfergus Castle, to which he laid siege. The castle soon surrendered, but only after the two rebellious barons had fled Ireland.

The castle was handed over to the care of John de Grey with orders to provision and garrison the castle for the King.

By the time King John left Ireland, Bishop John de Grey was in a more powerful position. He began a programme of castle building. He led an army to Athlone to suppress King Cathal of Connaught, who had been fiercely defending his independence and land from encroachment by Norman barons.

Bishop John, using his diplomatic skills, came to terms with the Irish King, persuaded him to sign a charter granting him the liberties of a baron. To contain King Cathal, castles were built at Athone and Clonmacnoise to protect important crossings on the river Shannon.

After the submission of Connaught he lead his army deep into the northern territory with the object of subduing the turbulent northern chieftains.

He easily routed the people of Fermanagh, and built castles at Clones and Narrow Water to use as bases from which he could strike north into Tirconnell.

The initial success of the expedition was soon frustrated by the fierce resistance from the clans of Tirconnell, led by Aedh O'Neill.

The Norman's and their allies were defeated by O'Neill, and the castle at Narrow Water was burned and the garrison slaughtered. Having repulsed 'the Foreign Bishop', Aedh O'Neill successfully maintained his independence throughout his 30 year rule.

Despite this setback John de Grey was not deterred from his mission, and diverted his attention to Meath where the titular king, Cormac, began to pose an active threat to the English settlers. The bishop met Cormac in battle near Kilnargram. Once again the bishop was out manoeuvred, and his army completely routed, even 'losing his horses, gold, silver, and other objects'.

Despite his military setbacks, John de Grey during his term as Viceroy of Ireland, abolished many native laws and replaced them with English laws. He also remodelled the Irish coinage on that of England.

THE DEATH OF ABBOT SAMSON

In spite of the bishops' cowardice the King's excommunication was widely published. But neither the excommunication or the interdict, which remained in force for many years and greatly effected the population, had virtually no effect on the irreligious King John, who was unmoved by the plight of his subjects.

Instead, he vented his anger by acts of wanton cruelty, particularly on clergymen who obeyed the interdict, and vowed to have Stephen Langton hanged if he set foot in England.

The Papal Bull of Excommunication had in effect absolved the barons from their oath of allegiance to him, therefore the potential threat of a rebellion caused King John to act swiftly against anyone showing signs of disloyalty,

When Geoffrey of Norwich, a clerk of the Exchequer, undoubtedly a religious man, refused to work in the service of the King whilst he was under excommunication, John's vengeance against him was one of extreme evil, he had Geoffrey dragged in chains to prison, where he was 'loaded with irons' and starved until he expired.

In 1211, the fourth year of the interdict, while the tyranny of the King continued unopposed, Abbot Samson of Bury St. Edmunds died at the age of 77. He had never been a particularly holy man, preferring politics and administration to his religious role, but had been devoted to the abbey, and had worked energetically to preserve the rights and privileges of the Liberty of St. Edmund.

He was greatly mourned by the monks of the abbey, who were saddened that his funeral ceremony was not allowed to take place inside the abbey church.

Because of the interdict they were obliged to carry his body to a meadow outside the abbey walls, and did so in silent reverence until they reached the plot of land where they buried him without the rights and ceremony of the church.

THE SIEGE OF BINHAM PRIORY

The Benedictine Priory of Binham stood in relative isolation on the uplands of North Norfolk. It had been founded as a cell of the Abbey of St. Albans, and perhaps because of its remoteness from the mother house, the priors were often less than holy men.

They were unscrupulous, irresponsible men, who wasted the priory's

Binham Priory, which was put under siege by FitzWalter in 1212. – EARLY TWENTIETH CENTURY POSTCARD.

income and coveted its silver for themselves. One such man was Prior Thomas, possibly a kinsman of Robert FitzWalter, the Lord of Dunmow, with whom he engaged a close friendship.

FitzWalter was a troublesome, quarrelsome adventurer, who had grown rich in the wine trade, and by an advantageous marriage to Lady Gunner, the grand-daughter of the founder of Binham Priory.

It may well have been Prior Thomas' close friendship and association with such a notorious character as FitzWalter that prompted the Abbot of St. Albans to dismiss him from his post. The dismissal of his friend outraged FitzWalter, who demanded that he be reinstated, which the Abbot refused to do.

There was, however, no limit to FitzWalter's skulduggery if he could not get his own way. He produced a deed, which gave him the patronage of the Priory and contained the proviso that a prior could not be removed from office without the consent of the patron, but the Abbot suspected the deed was a forgery and still refused to reinstate Thomas as prior.

Angered by the Abbot's intransigence, the headstrong FitzWalter gathered a force of troops and horsemen together and marched to Binham. There they encamped outside the priory and refused to let anyone enter or leave.

What FitzWalter hoped to gain by this action is not clear, but he kept the Priory under siege for several months. As supplies of food diminished inside, the monks were forced to eat bread made of bran and drink water from the drain pipes.

Realising that FitzWalter was not going to give up, the Abbot of St. Albans made sure that King John got to hear of the events at Binham.

Enraged by FitzWalter's audacity King John is said to have cried out, 'By God's feet, either I or FitzWalter must be King!' and immediately dispatched an army to relieve the Priory. But by the time his forces arrived at Binham, FitzWalter, having gained intelligence of the King's intention, had fled to France.

THE LORD OF DUNMOW'S DAUGHTER

Chroniclers of the time record that Robert FitzWalter, Lord of Dunmow, had a beautiful and chaste daughter named Matilda, whose beauty was widely renowned. It is said that King John himself fell in love with her and wanted her to become his mistress.

But Matilda rejected his advances and eventually fled to the safety of Sherwood Forest to escape his evil clutches. There she met the famed outlaw Robin Hood, and fell madly in love with him. She became known as 'Fair Maid Marion' to Robin's outlaw gang.

Matilda, 'The Fair Maid Marion,' lived with Robin and his outlaws, and shared their adventures for a few years, but when news reached her that her father had fled to France following the Binham Priory affair, she decided to return to Dunmow, and look after her father's estates.

When King John heard of the 'fair maid's' return, he resumed making his advances to her, but Matilda was in love with Robin, and ignored the love letters John sent to her.

The angry King was consumed with jealousy and decided that if he could not have her, then no-one else would. He sent a knight, Robert de Medewe to deliver her a bracelet as a token of his love. But unbeknown to Robert de Medewe, the bracelet was coated with a deadly poison.

When Robert was received by the 'fair maid' at Dunmow, he was dazzled by her beauty and stately appearance, and immediately fell in love with her. But he stifled his feelings and presented her with the King's gift, then left to return to the King's court in London.

Robert de Medewe could not forget the beautiful Matilda, or dismiss her from his mind. Overcome by his feelings he turned round and hurried back to Dunmow.

He arrived at Dunmow to find an ominous silence hanging over the place, and wondered why he was led into the Priory church. There to his horror he saw the lifeless body of the 'fair maid' laid on a bier and covered with flowers, the bracelet still on her wrist, the skin of her arm blackened by the poison. Robert was stricken with grief and mortified to think that he had been the unwitting instrument of her death. He refused to return to the court of

147

such an evil King as John, and decided to become a brother of the Order of St. Augustine and lived in a monastery for the rest of his life.

The 'fair maid' Matilda was laid to rest in a tomb in Dunmow Priory.

THE RETURN OF THE EXILES

The continued gloom of living under the interdict began to cause unrest, although the majority of the people thought the autocratic Pope had overstretched his powers, particularly in 1213 when he authorised King Philip of France to invade England, depose John and install his son Louis on the English throne.

King John's position became perilous when King Philip began preparing a huge fleet of ships to convey his invasion force to England, especially as he distrusted many of the barons, who, having been freed of their allegiance to him by the Pope, had openly declared their preference for Louis as king.

Fearful that he would lose the throne, John finally agreed to the Pope's terms, accepting Stephen Langton as Archbishop of Canterbury, granting peace and security to all who had been forced into exile, abolishing all bad laws and reviving the ancient laws of Edward the Confessor.

He also agreed to give freedom of election to the church, and to surrender his kingdom to the Pope and receive it back as a fief of Rome.

The Pope's legate, Pandulf Masca, together with Stephen Langton and Eustachius, Bishop of Ely, arrived at Dover on 13th May 1213. They were met by King John, who promised to uphold the conditions of his reconciliation with the Pope, and agreed that Bishop Eustachius, and all the other prelates whose estates he had confiscated, would be fully compensated.

Robert FitzWalter, Lord of Dunmow, also returned from exile a few days later. The King promised him safety, restored his Essex estates to him and 100 marks compensation, but the two men had a mutual hatred of each other, and neither of them greeted the occasion as one for forgiveness.

FitzWalter might eventually have got over his time in exile, but he could never overcome the bitterness he felt over the lecherous King's attempted seduction of his daughter, which had been the cause of her untimely death. He was to become King John's most vigorous opponent.

Earl William de Warenne, the King's relative, was charged by the Pope to ensure that King John observed his promises and that he governed the realm fair and justly.

But John had no intention of keeping his promises. He continued his harsh policies of imposing severe punishments on anyone who infringed the forest laws, high tax demands and heavy fines for petty misdemeanours. Little wonder that a chronicler of the time accused him of being the 'pillager of the people'.

THE BURY SCHISM

Once the interdict was lifted the monks of Bury St. Edmunds were able to retrieve the corpse of Abbot Samson from its makeshift grave in the meadow, and re-bury it with due ceremony in consecrated ground inside the abbey. They then set about electing a new Abbot.

As the Sacrist, Robert de Graveley, had virtually administered the affairs of the abbey throughout the interdict, and had done much improvement work on the abbey buildings, including the completion of the three great towers on the west front of the church, he naturally expected that he would be unanimously elected as Abbot.

But the monks were divided over their choice, and finally elected a young monk, Hugh de Northwold, from the cellerer's department, by a narrow majority, and duly submitted his name to King John for his approval.

King John, however, was angered because the monks had not continued the tradition of offering him the choice of three names from which he could choose. The position of Abbot was important, and he wanted it to be filled by a person who could be trusted to serve him, and therefore refused to recognise the election of Hugh as Abbot.

His refusal threw the abbey into confusion, and resulted in bitter rivalry between the monks who accepted the King's right to choose, led by Robert de Graveley, and those who favoured a free election as promised by the King on his submission to the Pope, not surprisingly led by Hugh de Northwold.

To settle the schism, King John requested the intervention of the Pope's newly appointed Legate to England, Nicholas, Bishop of Tusculum, who arrived at Bury just before Christmas 1213.

He took over the administration of the abbey, but was in no hurry to bring the dispute to an end for as long as the abbacy remained vacant the revenues from its extensive estates went in to the ever-greedy King's treasury.

Hugh de Northwold, Abbot of Bury St Edmunds, depicted on the abbey's Great Seal.

149

Frustrated by the uncertainty of his position in the abbey, Hugh de Northwold decided that the best way to settle the dispute was to travel to Rome and appeal directly to Pope Innocent to support his candidacy. But disappointingly for Hugh the Pope appeared to have more important matters to decide, and Hugh was forced to return to England with the issue still unresolved.

THE KING AT FRAMLINGHAM CASTLE

King John's humiliating submission to the Pope made him appear a weak monarch, and did not diffuse the crisis with many of his barons. Consequently the allegiance of many of the barons remained doubtful and John wondered just whom he could trust.

After much pondering over past records, John decided that of all the East Anglian magnates Roger Bigod, the powerful Earl of Norfolk, was the most likely to be disloyal to him. So he concluded that somehow he must win the support of Bigod, and decided to pay him a visit.

The news that the King intended to visit the Bigods' made the Earl and his wife, Countess Ida, hastily re-organise life at their chief castle at Framlingham to accommodate the King and his large entourage, and ensure that he enjoyed the lavish style to which he was accustomed.

The newly completed castle at Framlingham was built on the site of the old castle that had been demolished after the first earl's rebellion in 1174. It was an impressive stronghold with 13 towers and thick masonry walls,

Framlingham Castle, the fortress home of Roger Bigod.

incorporating the latest in defence design, and was a fitting residence for a powerful baron, but it had been rebuilt without a Royal License.

Earl Bigod must have been concerned by his neglect to secure royal approval for his castle, but no doubt hoped that the up-to-date kitchens would supply the greedy, food-loving King with a good supply of mouth-watering delicacies that would well compensate for such a small misdemeanour.

King John was obsessed with personal cleanliness and took baths regularly, employing his own personal bathman, who travelled everywhere with him. The designers of Framlingham had not considered the need for anything other than basic sanitation, as etiquette required the washing of face and hands every morning, a bath was only taken in extreme cases for reasons of health when prescribed by a doctor. The King, as at most places, would have to make do with a wooden tub.

But whatever went on behind the massive walls of Framlingham Castle, the King departed presumably satisfied that he had won Bigod's loyalty. But, despite his outward display of cordiality, Bigod, was neither impressed with the King's obsession with hygiene nor with his qualities of leadership.

DEATH OF A FIGHTING BISHOP

John was anxious to prove to his barons that he was a strong leader and that his nickname, 'Softsword', was unjustified. He planned to reconquer his continental possessions that had been lost to France, particularly his ancestral homelands of Anjou and Normandy.

A war on the continent would also keep the barons occupied, leaving them little time to plot against him. But when John called them to do service many refused to join him or send their knights and soldiers, claiming that their feudal obligation was to defend the realm and not participate in adventurous, aggressive wars on the continent. To further anger the King many barons would not pay scutage in lieu of service.

John was undeterred by this reaction. His treasury was full, enabling him to raise an army, which according to one chronicler, consisted of a 'few earls, but an infinite multitude of low-class soldiers of fortune'. He was joined by his half-brother, William of Salisbury, and John de Grey, Bishop of Norwich, who brought over from Ireland '5000 knights and horsemen' to swell his forces.

King John had also formed an alliance with his nephew, Emperor Otto IV of Germany, who had agreed to attack France from the north so that the French would have to fight invasions on two fronts.

The invasions went ahead, and the King's campaign in Southern France went well at first. Within a month 26 castles had been taken, including the fortress town of Angers, the 'capital' of his forebears, and also the town of

Robert FitzWalter, rallying the barons to rebellion against King John, before the Shrine of St Edmund. – EARLY TWENTIETH CENTURY POSTCARD.

Rochfort, which was captured by the Bishop of Norwich. But in the north, Otto, supported by William of Salisbury and hordes of Flemish mercenaries, made disappointing headway.

King John's victories in the south were soon reversed when the French began a counter offensive. Prince Louis defeated the Bishop of Norwich's forces and re-took many of the castles. The greatest defeat, which brought an end to the whole campaign, was on 14th July when the King of France utterly defeated Emperor Otto at the Battle of Bouvines.

King John's dream of reconquering his continental provinces was shattered and he was forced to make a humiliating truce with King Philip. He returned to England and would never again meddle in continental affairs, but his troubles were by no means over.

Despite Bishop John de Grey's unwavering support for King John during the interdict, Pope Innocent considered de Grey the best person to fill the vacant Bishopric of Durham. So no sooner had he returned to England from the wars in France than he was summoned to Rome by the Pope.

He undertook the long journey, only to find when he arrived in Rome that the monks from Durham had preceded him and had informed the Pope that they were unwilling to accept his proposed candidate and had put forward their own nominee.

Bishop de Grey, left the monks and the Pope to argue it out. No doubt worn out by his arduous life, he set off for home, but only got as far as the French town of St. John de Angelo, near Poitiers, when he was taken ill, and died there on the 18th October 1214. His body was conveyed back to Norwich, where it was buried in the presbytery of the cathedral.

THE MEETING OF THE BARONS

While the King was campaigning on the Continent, Peter des Roches, Bishop of Winchester, acted as Regent, and although he had no experience in legal matters, he also became Chief Justiciar following the death of Geoffrey FitzPeter.

A Frenchman from Poitou, des Roches was unpopular with the English barons because of his aggressive, intolerant and dictatorial manner, and became known as the 'Warrior of Winchester'. A chronicler of the time remarked that he was 'keen on accounting, slack at scripture'.

To ensure the King's army in France was supplied with food, weapons and mercenaries, des Roches imposed a scutage, known as the Poitou Scutage. It was the heaviest tax of all ever imposed on the barons, and resentment grew against the continuous demands for tax and services.

When King John returned to England after his defeat by the French King, he found the barons in a rebellious mood, especially in the North and in East Anglia. Unbeknown to him, Robert FitzWalter, Lord of Dunmow, who despised the King, had called a secret meeting of the barons at Bury St. Edmunds Abbey.

The King not only feared a revolt by the barons, but also an invasion by the King of France. Knowing that East Anglia was a hotbed of resistance, he thought it wise to ensure that the royal castles were still in the safe hands of loyal constables, and first visited Colchester Castle to ensure the loyalty of its constable, William de Lanvalei.

The Lanvalei family had held the Constableship of the Castle for three generations and had served their monarch faithfully, but William, who also held the Barony of Laxdon, resented the King's high tax demands, even though he did not express his feelings during the King's visit.

As soon as the King departed, Lanvalei placed his deputy, Matthew Mantel, in charge of the castle and rode off to Bury St. Edmunds to attend the meeting of the barons, which was held on the 20th November 1214.

Many leading barons of East Anglia assembled at Bury, including Richard de Clare, Geoffrey de Manderville Earl of Essex, Roger Bigod, Earl of Norfolk, Robert de Vere, Earl of Oxford, and William de Huntingfield, Sheriff of Norfolk and Suffolk.

Meeting before the shrine of St. Edmund, the barons discussed the Charter of Henry I, which contained laws and liberties granted to the church and nobles of England. They all agreed that King John and his henchmen had abused most of these laws and liberties.

Consequently, led by Robert FitzWalter, they each swore on the High Altar that if the King did not grant them their rightful liberties they would withdraw their allegiance and make war on him. They each agreed to arm for war and put their demands to the King after Christmas.

Meanwhile, when King John learned of Lanvalei's treachery, he immediately sent Stephen Herengoot, a Flemish freebooter with an army of mercenaries to Colchester to evict Lanvalei's deputy, Matthew Mantel, from the castle.

At the sight of the huge mercenary army, Mantel surrendered without a fight, and Herengoot took possession of the castle. Herengoot began to strengthen the fortress and prepare it for a siege. To give the castle a better defence against a siege, two siege engines, balistas, huge powerful crossbows that could shoot five foot long armour-piercing javelins, which had the velocity to transfix three men at a time, were fixed on the castle parapets, and trained engineers in operating them were brought from London. Colchester was now securely in the hands of the King.

MAGNA CARTA

King John had little choice but to meet the barons, and did so in London on 6th January 1215. They asked him to confirm the Charter of Henry I and restore the laws of Edward the Confessor, and he promised to give them an answer by Easter.

The barons agreed to wait until then without realising that John was playing for time to raise another mercenary army. In the meantime, he appealed to Pope Innocent III for help, vowing to go on a crusade. The Pope responded by telling the barons that they must obey their King and pay his tax demands.

When they received this order from the Pope, the infuriated barons fully armed themselves and mustered at Stamford on 19th April 1215. They first requested another meeting with the King, who refused to attend. Whereupon Robert FitzWalter, who had no interest in the Charter, but thirsted for the King's blood, was elected supreme leader of the rebel army, taking the title, Marshal of the Army of God and the Holy Church.

They marched to Northampton with the intention of taking the Royal Castle. However, after besieging it for two weeks without success, they realised that the castle was so well-defended and moved on to Bedford Castle where they thought they would have more success.

Success also eluded them at Bedford, so they moved on again to London, where the supporters of the barons opened the gates of the city. FitzWalter took control of the City, with the exception of the Tower of London, where loyal supporters of the King held out.

King John remained in safety behind the strong walls of Windsor Castle while the trouble continued, until Archbishop Langton, who was trusted by both sides, tried to arrange a truce and negotiate terms that would be acceptable to the King and the barons.

Even while negotiations were taking place, King John awaited a massive army of mercenaries from Poitou, under the leadership of Savaric de Mauleon, a notorious freebooter, to enable him to regain control of the country, but on the 10th June 1215 he was forced to agree to a draft charter, which became known as the Magna Carta, giving the church and nobility the liberties they had demanded.

King John also agreed to meet the barons at Runnymede on the 15th June.

RUNNYMEDE

Ever since his disputed election as Abbot of Bury St. Edmunds, Hugh de Northwold had made further efforts to persuade the King to recognise his election. But while the King was enjoying the profits of the abbey he was in no hurry to fill the vacancy.

The abbey was one of the largest landowners in East Anglia and also exercised certain feudal and military obligations, so the crisis with the rebellious barons brought the matter to a head.

It was now important to the King that the vacancy of abbot was filled with a trusted and loyal person, so he summoned Hugh de Northwold to meet him at Runnymede prior to his meeting with the barons, which he did.

At this meeting King John agreed to accept Hugh as abbot with the promise that he could also act as Sheriff and collect the royal dues, as the official Sheriff had thrown in his lot with the rebels. Hugh must have agreed to the King's conditions because he returned to Bury St. Edmunds as undisputed abbot. The following day King John met his barons at Runnymede and reluctantly put his seal to the Magna Carta, in the presence of Archbishop Langton, Robert FitzWalter, Roger Bigod, and all the other rebellious barons.

THE ROAD TO CIVIL WAR

After the Magna Carta had been signed and sealed by the King, the barons returned to their castles, satisfied that any lands they held that had been illegally confiscated by the monarch would be returned as rightfully theirs. They remained in a state of readiness for war, however, as they still did not completely trust the King.

Their precautionary measures were well justified as King John had grudgingly signed the Charter but had no intention of observing it. He felt in a strong position, having the support of his half-brother, William of Salisbury, and kinsman William de Warenne, as well as several other barons from the South and West.

He could also rely on the mercenary forces from Poitou, under the command of Savaric de Mauleon, and was expecting more mercenaries from Flanders, under the command of Hugh de Bovas, to land in Kent. But things went terribly wrong with the fleet of ships bringing them to England.

A sudden, violent storm blew up and wrecked most of the ships. It was said that 40,000 bodies of men, women and children were washed up along the shores of Norfolk and Suffolk. According to one chronicler, 'the very air was tainted with the stench of rotting corpses'. The body of Hugh de Bovas was washed ashore near Great Yarmouth.

When King John was given the tragic news of the loss of his mercenary army he was seized with a dreadful rage and 'remained until the evening as if he were possessed by madness'.

He continued to brood over events until September 1215 when he sent a message to Pope Innocent III asking him to annul the Charter. This was a direct violation of Clause 61 of the Charter, and was the excuse FitzWalter, who was one of the appointed guardians of the Charter, needed to rally the barons for war.

As the East Anglian barons garrisoned their castles and mustered their forces, the Pope sent orders that all 'Disturbers of the Kingdom of England' should be excommunicated and their lands placed under an interdict.

King John was satisfied that the Pope's reply would put an end to the unrest, but the Pope's orders were of little deterrent to the barons. who were now determined to rid England of its tyrannical King, FitzWalter declaring that the 'King was the greatest disturber of the peace'.

THE PILLAGE OF EAST ANGLIA

With the inevitable outbreak of civil war, the King's forces kept FitzWalter pent-up in London while Savaric de Mauleon and his mercenaries marched into East Anglia, burning and looting villages as they made their way to Pleshey Castle, the seat of Geoffrey de Manderville, Earl of Essex.

After laying waste to the surrounding countryside, they seized the castle on Christmas Eve 1215, and took it with ease. Flushed with success they moved on to Tilty Abbey, arriving on Christmas Day just as Mass was being celebrated.

Heedless of the sacred occasion they broke down the gates and stormed into the abbey, looting and destroying everything they could lay their hands on. In spite of being taken by surprise, the monks put up a brave fight to save their church from further destruction, but many were killed during the process, and the mercenaries plundered the church of its gold and silver objects before leaving.

Loaded with booty, Savaric de Mauleon, who was now known by the nickname of Savaric the Bloody, marched on to Colchester Castle. William de Lanvalei, who had regained control of the castle after the signing of the Magna Carta, had been kept informed of the mercenaries progress across Essex, and had increased the garrison and prepared the balistas, left by Herengoot, in readiness for a siege. The castle was so-well defended that the odds seemed to be in Lanvalei's favour. But de Mauleon had also brought siege engines with him. Included in their arsenal were large and powerful missile throwing machines, known as trebuchet, which could throw huge 15kg stone balls with deadly effect.

While Colchester Castle was under siege, King John divided his forces leaving some to guard London, while he led the other half to Framlingham Castle with the intention of bringing Bigod to account. Bigod had, however, fled from the castle and joined the barons' army, leaving Framlingham in the care of William de Enveise, one of his tenants.

Garrisoned by 26 knights, 20 sergeants and 7 crossbowmen, the castle was well prepared for a siege, but the defenders were unwilling to endure a long siege, and after a feeble resistance, de Enveise negotiated a surrender.

The King took control of the castle, appointed Elvas de Beauchamp as custodian, confiscated Bigod's lands and deprived him of the Barony of Framlingham.

From Framlingham King John marched to Colchester, where Savaric de Mauleon was still struggling to break down the walls of the castle against fierce opposition from the besieged. The siege had raged with such velocity that a chronicler later commented that 'there had been no siege in those days more earnestly enforced, nor more obstinately defended'.

157

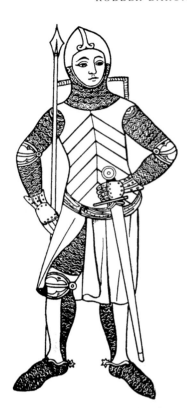

Gilbert de Clare, Earl of Hertford, one of the leading rebel barons who supported Prince Louis.

But the ceaseless bombardment of huge missiles continued to rain down on the castle walls. Eventually part of the wall was reduced to rubble, and William de Lanvalei and his garrison were forced to retreat to the massive keep, where they continued to hold out. It was not the missiles of de Mauleon that ultimately forced them to surrender, but famine.

King John, allowed the garrison to evacuate the castle, the flag of the Lanvalei's was pulled down, and the castle was once again put under the care of Stephen Herengoot.

The King and his army them moved on to Hedingham Castle, which Robert de Vere, Earl of Oxford, was holding. They immediately laid siege to the castle and quickly broke through the curtain wall. After three days, de Vere, having no desire for a long and damaging siege, surrendered, and was given safe conduct to leave his castle.

With Hedingham securely under his authority, the King then assessed his situation. As most of East Anglia was now under his control he decided to return to London, where FitzWalter and a large contingent of rebels held out.

THE PLUNDER OF ELY

Meanwhile, many East Anglian rebels had fled to the Island of Ely, where they fortified the old Ely Castle, and thought themselves secure in the 'Camp of Refuge'. But the weather in early 1216 turned bitterly cold with severe frosts that froze the water and marshes surrounding the island.

The ice thickened to such an extent that the King's mercenaries were able to cross it and reach the island as if they were treading solid ground. Walter Buck and his band of Brabant freebooters, crossed from Earith, while a party of Flemings, under the command of the fierce and murderous Falkes de Breaute, crossed over the ice from Stuntney and attacked the island.

The combined forces soon overcome all resistance, capturing 15 knights and destroying the castle. Many of the knights of noble rank attempted to escape, but were soon captured and submitted to torture until they agreed to pay a ransom to secure their release.

Described as an 'unscrupulous and godless man', Falkes de Breaute and his soldiers entered Ely Cathedral 'with drawn swords', and, after plundering the place, they seized Prior Roger de Brigham and threatened to burn the building down unless he paid them 200 marks in silver.

The freebooters then went on the rampage in the countryside around Ely, plundering, killing, burning churches and laying waste to everything until, satisfied with their spoils, they departed leaving the whole island devastated.

THE INVASION OF PRINCE LOUIS

With most of East Anglia now firmly under Royal control and the rebel barons, who were denounced by the Pope as 'worse than Saracens', trapped in London, King John considered himself once again in command of his Kingdom.

Robert FitzWalter had, however, slipped over to France, cursing the King for subjecting the land to the fire and sword of ignoble foreigners, and taking a special message from the barons for Prince Louis of France offering him the throne of England.

Prince Louis gladly accepted the offer, seeing it as an excuse to invade England, and raised an army in preparation for crossing the Channel. When King John gained news of Prince Louis' invasion plans, he gave orders to all South and Eastern coastal towns, including King's Lynn, Great Yarmouth and Dunwich, that they were to send warships to intercept Prince Louis' fleet. The English fleet were ordered to assemble at Dover in readiness to repel the invasion.

But during the night of 18th May 1216. a severe gale blew most of the ships on to the shore, leaving them hopelessly stranded, and Prince Louis was able to cross the Channel unopposed when the gale abated. His huge army landed at Sandwich, Kent, and marched on London where they were received with jubilation by the barons who were freed from their confinement in London.

Although most of the castles still remained in the hands of King John, he was forced to retreat to the West Country to consolidate his support, while Robert FitzWalter, supported by Gilbert de Clare, Earl of Hertford, and William de Huntingfield, the former Sheriff of Suffolk, took a powerful force of knights, men at arms, and general rabble into Suffolk and Essex to bring the counties under the subjection of Prince Louis.

Although they failed to recapture any of the castles they once again subjected the countryside to rampage and pillage.

TRAGEDY IN THE WASH

By the beginning of September 1216 King John had rallied enough support to make a major offensive against the rebels. Mustering his forces at Oxford, he decided to march on Cambridge hoping to trap and defeat the King of Scots, who, having taken advantage of the civil strife, invaded England and had penetrated as far south as Cambridge with his army.

King John took Cambridge surprisingly easy, only to find that the Scots had retreated north to Lincoln. Leaving Cambridge in the hands of Falkes de Breaute, John marched on through Huntingdon, spreading terror amongst the inhabitants as he pursued the retreating Scots.

When he reached Peterborough, he plundered the town. Before pressing on to Lincoln he ordered Savaric de Mauleon to arrest some rebel knights who had sought sanctuary in Crowland Abbey.

Savaric and his men-at-arms entered the Abbey church, violently dragged the rebel knights out, then plundered the abbey and threatened to burn it down unless the monks paid a large ransom. The monks paid the ransom to save their abbey from further destruction and Savaric left them in peace.

By the time King John reached Lincoln, the Scots had retreated even further north, and he sought a much needed rest at Lincoln Castle, where he was warmly welcomed by his loyal custodian, Dame Nicola de la Haye, who entertained him lavishly throughout his stay.

During his respite at Lincoln he decided not to continue his pursuit of the Scots, but to seek revenge on the rebels of East Anglia, so returned south-east to King's Lynn, where the town's burgesses, who were anxious to save the town from plunder, welcomed him and treated him to a sumptuous feast.

The greedy monarch could not resist the numerous courses of succulent food served to him, and over-indulged, with the result that he suffered a bout of dysentery.

In spite of his discomfort, the King was anxious to get on the road again and, when he had partly recovered, he set off for Wisbech with his army and baggage train on the 11th October 1216.

They decided to take a short cut and cross the wide estuary of the River Ouse at low tide without realising the dangers.

The huge, heavy wagons soon ran into difficulties, sinking into the treacherous quicksands, which, according to one chronicler, 'sucked in everything, including men and horses'.

The disaster quickly turned into a major tragedy as the fast incoming tide overwhelmed them. King John, and the majority of his knights, escaped, but 'he lost all his carts, wagons and baggage horses, together with his money, costly vessels and everything which he had particular regard for'.

It was believed that among the items that sank into the quicksands was the

Prince Louis of France invaded and occupied East Anglia in his attempt to seize the Crown of England.

royal regalia, including the imperial crown of his grandmother, the Empress Maud.

The King, suffering from fever, arrived at Swineshead Abbey, where the monks attended to his every need. Aware of his gluttonous appetite, they feasted him generously. It was said that, in spite of his condition, the King surfeited himself with peaches and drinking new cider which inevitably worsened his condition.

On the following day, although weak and in pain, the King insisted on travelling to the Bishop of Lincoln's castle at Newark, even though he was in no condition to ride, but managed the journey in considerable discomfort.

When he arrived at the castle he was in such a state, the Abbot of Croxton, 'a man skilled in medicine' was immediately called to attend him. Apart from bleeding him there was nothing else the abbot could do as the King's condition worsened, and he died on the 19th October 1216.

THE FLEUR DE LYS OVER EAST ANGLIA
Prince Louis controlled London at the time of King John's death, and would have been crowned king had he been able to find an English bishop who was willing to perform the ceremony.

But all the bishops who had supported the barons against King John, now gave their allegiance to his nine-year-old son Henry, who was crowned King at Bristol, and the Earl of Pembroke was chosen to act as Regent during the new King's minority.

Prince Louis then decided to establish control over the whole of Eastern England, and began by taking control of the royal castle at Hertford, which he handed over to Robert FitzWalter. His army then marched into East Anglia, where he easily re-took Castle Hedingham and returned it to Robert de Vere.

The Castle of Colchester was taken after the garrison was handsomely bribed into surrendering. From Colchester, Prince Louis marched on to Norwich where the castle was held for the King by Thomas de Burgh, who was under orders to hold and defend it at all costs.

But when the cowardly de Burgh saw the victorious army of Prince Louis approaching he lost his nerve and fled, leaving the garrison to do whatever they thought best. After Prince Louis allowed his soldiers to plunder and terrorise the townsfolk, the garrison decided that it would be unwise to try and defend the castle and surrendered it to the rebels.

The Fleur de Lys now flew from all the royal castles in East Anglia.

THE GRAND THEFT

Hugh de Northwold, Abbot of Bury St. Edmunds, tried to steer clear of the troubles between King John and the barons, spending most of his time attempting to persuade the King to accept his election as abbot.

Following King John's death, Hugh considered it wise to seek confirmation of his position by paying homage to the young King Henry and so keep on the right side of his powerful Regent, a course of action which paid off as he was eventually recognised as the Abbot of Bury St. Edmunds.

While Hugh was absent from the abbey, Prince Louis ordered Viscount de Meleun to visit the abbey with a small contingent of knights, not with orders to plunder it of its precious gold and silver treasures, but on a secret mission to acquire the remains of St. Edmund.

The purpose of their mission was kept secret from the monks, who would never freely part with such a revered and treasured relic. The Viscount had to acquire it by stealth, undoubtedly with the connivance and possibly the bribery of a senior member of the abbey.

Although there is no direct proof, Robert de Graveley, the sacristan, must be a prime suspect. He had disputed the election of Hugh de Northwold as abbot, and was bitter that, having done so much for the abbey, he had not been elected.

The remains of St. Edmund were secretly removed and hidden in the Viscount's baggage wagon when he left the abbey. Later, Robert de Graveley secured promotion by being appointed Abbot of Thorney, taking the secret of the Saint's removal from Bury with him, no doubt smugly satisfied that Hugh de Northwold ruled an abbey with an empty shrine. It was many years before the loss was discovered.

THE DEFEAT OF FITZWALTER

By Christmas Prince Louis was in control of Cambridge, and decided to call a council of his supporters with the object of arranging a truce and agreeing peace terms with Regent Pembroke. A meeting consequently took place, and, although no peace terms were arranged they agreed a truce should last a few months as neither side appeared to be winning the struggle.

Prince Louis took advantage of the lull in military activity by returning to Calais in February 1217, and was pleased to find that his wife, Blanche of Castile, had mustered a large army of reinforcements during his absence.

But while he was absent from England, many barons who had supported him had second thoughts and deserted his cause, conscious that they had a duty to support the rightful King of England and drive out the French invaders. Robert FitzWalter, however, stubbornly remained firmly loyal to Prince Louis.

FitzWalter was defeated at Lincoln.

Prince Louis returned to England in April 1217 with the reinforcements. In an attempt to improve his fortunes, he made what was to prove a monumental mistake by deciding to split his army into two forces.

One part under his command, would attack Dover, while the other part, mainly consisting of rebels and French mercenaries under the command of FitzWalter, would attack Lincoln Castle, which still held out in support of King Henry.

FitzWalter led his army north, 'pillaging in the usual custom', as one chronicler recorded, 'the soldiers of the French Kingdom being as it were the refuse and scum of that country, left nothing at all untouched'.

At Lincoln they laid siege to the castle and 'made fierce assaults on the castle, whilst the besieged returned their showers of stone and missiles with great courage'.

While the siege was going on the Regent Pembroke gathered a huge army at Newark and they began their march to Lincoln on the sixth day of Whitsun 1217. When FitzWalter observed Pembroke's army approaching he decided to hold his ground believing he had the superior force, but had not considered the deadly skill of the Regent's crossbow.

By their precision 'the horses of the barons were mown down like pigs'. Many of the barons were taken prisoner, while the French mercenaries took flight. FitzWalter, and Gilbert de Clare, Earl of Hertford, were two of the 300 knights who were taken prisoner.

When Prince Louis heard of FitzWalter's crushing defeat at Lincoln he knew his cause was lost, and that he had no choice but surrender London to the Regent. Under an amnesty he returned to France, with the remains of St. Edmund still hidden in his baggage wagon.

Surprisingly FitzWalter, who had been the chief instigator of the rebellion, was treated leniently, and his Essex estates were eventually restored to him.

The Fleur de Lys was taken down and replaced with the royal standard over the royal castles. East Anglia was once again fully under the control of the rightful King of England, Henry III.

Places to Visit

Whilst every effort has been made to ensure the information in this section is correct, Opening times and charges frequently change. You are therefore advised to check with the local Tourist Information Centre before planning a visit.

BINHAM PRIORY
Remains of the Priory besieged by Fitzwalter, part of which now serves as a parish church.

Open: any reasonable time
Admission: free

BUNGAY CASTLE AND VISITOR CENTRE
Remains of Roger Bigod's stronghold, with unique siege mine under the keep. The visitor centre contains a model of the castle.

Open: times not known
Admission: charge

BURY ST EDMUNDS ABBEY
Abbey ruins set in attractive gardens.

Open: any reasonable time
Admission: free

CASTLE ACRE CASTLE
Remains of William de Warenne's castle, with impressive earthworks.

Open: any reasonable time
Admission: free

CASTLE ACRE PRIORY
Remains of the Cluniac Priory founded by William de Warenne, with a well preserved Prior's house.

Open: daily 10.00–17.00
Admission: charge

CASTLE RISING CASTLE
Large Norman keep, home of the de Albini family.

Open: daily 10.00–17.00
Admission: charge

COLCHESTER CASTLE MUSEUM
Largest Norman keep in England containing a museum with audio visual dramas explaining Colchester's history.

Open: daily 10.00–17.00. Sunday 13.00–17.00
Admission: charge

ELY CATHEDRAL
Norman Cathedral with a superb Lantern lower.

Open: daily 07.30–18.00
Admission: charge except Sundays

FRAMLINGHAM CASTLE
Remains of Roger Bigod's castle.

Open: daily 10.00–17.00
Admission: charge

HEDINGHAM CASTLE
Superb Norman keep, built for Aubrey the Grim, with one of the finest Norman arches in England.

Open: daily April–October 10.00–17.00
Admission: charge

LINCOLN CASTLE
Houses one of only four original surviving copies of the Magna Carta.

Open: daily all year round 09.30–17.30 Monday–Saturday, 11.00–17.30 Sundays. Closes at 16.00 during winter months. Closed Christmas Day, Boxing Day and New Year's Day.
Admission: charge

MOUNTFITCHET CASTLE, STANSTED
Reconstructed Norman castle and village on original site.

Open: daily March–November 10.00–17.00
Admission: charge

NORWICH CASTLE MUSEUM

Large restored Norman keep containing a museum.

Open: all year Monday–Saturday 10.00–17.00
Admission: charge

NORWICH CATHEDRAL

Fine cathedral begun by Herbert de Losinga.

Open: daily 07.30–18.00
Admission: free

ORFORD CASTLE

Unusually designed keep built for King Henry II.

Open: daily 10.00–17.00
Admission: charge

PETERBOROUGH CATHEDRAL AND VISITOR CENTRE

Norman cathedral, formerly the church of Peterborough Abbey.

Open: daily 07.30–17.15
Admission: charge

WALTHAM ABBEY

Remains of abbey serving as a parish church. Burial place of King Harold.

Open: daily 10.00–16.00
Admission: free

WYMONDHAM ABBEY

Remains of abbey serving as the parish church.

Open: any reasonable time
Admission: free

Index

172

About the Authors

Derek Richings and Roger Rudderham worked together on two previous books: *Littleport in Old Picture Postcards* and *Strange Tales of East Anglia*. Roger, who currently lives in Cambridge, is an experienced and enthusiastic researcher of local history. Derek was born in Peterborough, and after many years living in the London area, settled in Littleport, where he became (with Roger) one of the founder members of the Littleport Society. Apart from a lifelong interest in writing, Derek enjoyed singing and playing the classical guitar. Sadly, he died in 2001 before completing his work on *Robber Barons and Fighting Bishops*, so the book was brought through its final stages by his wife, Brenda, and son, Darrell.

Acknowledgements

We would like to acknowledge the help given by the staff of the Cambridge City Library, the Suffolk Record Office, Bury St Edmunds, the Norwich City Library, and the Saffron Walden Library. Also special thanks to Brenda Richings and Darrell Richings for their hard work in putting the typescript in order and for proof reading.

We also thank the Cambridgeshire Collection, Cambridge City Library, for allowing us to reproduce illustrations from their collection. Every effort has been made to trace any other copyright holders, but if infringement of copyright has been unintentionally made we apologise and corrections will be made in future editions.